T0243929

PRAISE FOR *MINI BIG IDEAS*

'A joyful romp through the history of civilisation,
full of snackable curiosities.'

Tim Harford, author of *How to Make the World Add Up*

'Who knew that the biggest ideas in the universe could fit in such a small
package? *Mini Big Ideas* is a delightful introduction to some of the most
profound discoveries and open questions in science and philosophy. A fun
and inspiring teaser for curious minds that will fit in your purse, or your
man-purse, or whatever you use to carry stuff around with you.'

Jérémie Harris, author of *Quantum Physics Made Me Do It*

'Like fitting an elephant into a thimble, Jonny Thomson manages
to cram some of the world's biggest, grandest ideas into only a few
hundred words. Witty, knowledgeable and mind-expanding.'

Richard Fisher, author of *The Long View*

Jonny Thomson taught philosophy in Oxford for more than a decade before turning to writing full-time. He's a staff writer at Big Think, where he writes about philosophy, theology, psychology and occasionally other subjects when he dares step out of his lane. His first book, *Mini Philosophy*, is an award-winning, international bestseller, and has been translated into twenty languages. Jonny also runs the 'Mini Philosophy' Instagram and Facebook accounts (@philosophyminis).

Jonny lives in Oxfordshire with his wife, who is very helpful, and his two young boys, who are not.

PRAISE FOR *MINI PHILOSOPHY*

'Engaging, smart and wise, *Mini Philosophy* is a diverse taster menu of ideas on life, the mind and the world.'

David Mitchell, author of *Cloud Atlas* and *The Bone Clocks*

'A neat idea, deftly executed. If this doesn't light your philosophical fuse, you don't have one.'

Dr Julian Baggini, Academic Director, Royal Institute of Philosophy

'Each one of these sparkling pieces is a delight to read, without ever compromising on substance.'

Oliver Burkeman, author of *Four Thousand Weeks*

Mini
Big
Ideas

A Little Book of
Big Innovations

Jonny Thomson

WILDFIRE

First published in 2023 by
WILDFIRE
an imprint of HEADLINE PUBLISHING GROUP

1

Cataloguing in Publication Data is available from the British Library

Hardback ISBN 978 1 4722 9856 0

Typeset in Gotham by Seagulls.net

Printed and bound in Great Britain by Clays Ltd, Elcograf S.p.A.

Headline's policy is to use papers that are natural, renewable and recyclable products and made from wood grown in well-managed forests and other controlled sources. The logging and manufacturing processes are expected to conform to the environmental regulations of the country of origin.

HEADLINE PUBLISHING GROUP
An Hachette UK Company
Carmelite House
50 Victoria Embankment
London EC4Y 0DZ

www.headline.co.uk
www.hachette.co.uk

To Charlie,
who will, one day, change the world

Contents

MEDICINE

SOCIETY

Introduction

L. P. Hartley once wrote, 'The past is a foreign country; they do things differently there.' He was right: the people of yesterday dressed weirdly and they talked in funny ways. But, more importantly, they had an utterly alien way of seeing the world. It's the nature of human psychology to assume the 'now' is the norm. We've become so used to our modern technology and our modern ideologies that it's incredibly hard – impossible, perhaps – to entirely relate to the 'Before Time'.

Yet I still enjoy imagining what it was like. That moment, a very long time ago, when someone, somewhere, turned up to dinner saying, 'Hey guys, what do you think of this "wheel" idea?' It's a curious thing, but humans actually managed quite well before the wheel. If you have a few minutes spare, try to picture the 'Before Time'. Imagine a world without clocks, monotheism or antibiotics. A life without plastics, marriage or the nation-state. Take any 'big idea' from these pages and try to picture how your day-to-day life would have worked without it. For some ideas, this is easier to imagine. Many reading this will remember the 'Before Time' of an internet-free age (although you might find it hard to remember how you did a lot of things). For other ideas, though, this is harder to grasp. How could people *not* know about germs?

How did people not know about the elements? How did anyone get by without writing, money or electricity?

My definition of a 'big idea' is something that pops up and swells so far as to entirely occupy the zeitgeist of the time. It doesn't necessarily mean that it's a paradigm shift, but it's definitely an idea that recalibrates and reorientates society. Ideas like evolution, the combustion engine and banking lifted the world up, shook it about a bit and placed it back down looking different to how it was before. Big ideas are those that have a 'Before Time'.

Like every generation since the dawn of mankind, we've our own big ideas to deal with today. It could be gene editing, nanotechnology, artificial intelligence or quantum physics, but *something* is going to define our times. Some of these are disruptive ideas; some are so innovative we initially find them disturbing.

I hope *Mini Big Ideas* does two things. First, I want it to be a fun and light-hearted way to help you learn more about those ideas you've always wanted to understand. Second, it's a book of hope – because humans have dealt with revolutionary technologies and innovations for millennia, and we're still here. Our species has lived through hundreds of 'This changes everything!' moments, only to find that, actually, we simply adapt, adjust and carry on. But we do have an easier time pushing a supermarket trolley now we've figured out the concept of wheels.

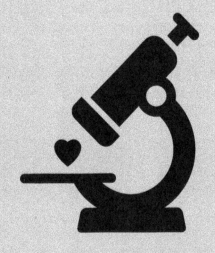

Biology

Biology is the study of living things, from tiny amino acids to magnificent blue whales. It's about a dense canopy of jungle and lakes covered in algae. It's about bacteria fighting an immune system; predators and prey; birth and death. The future of biology is, of course, the future of us. As we peer into a tomorrow of CRISPR, gene editing and nanotechnology, we're going to need many more biologists.

Biology is about that most remarkable and magical of phenomena: life.

The Origins of Life
The First Flick of the Evolutionary Domino

Let's step into a time machine to go back 4 billion years. As you exit in your sleek and surprisingly flattering time-suit, you gasp at the hellscape before you. Earth as you know it is almost unrecognisable: there are five-hour days, a huge moon and great volcanic islands spewing magma. The oceans are at a bubbling, angry boil and meteorites are smashing all around. The small amount of oxygen available is tied up in compounds and is certainly not found in the air. It's here, somewhere, that we will find the origins of life.

Up until the last few decades, the most popular origin-of-life idea was known as the 'primordial soup' hypothesis. It goes back to the 1950s, when Stanley Miller and Harold Urey reproduced in the laboratory what they thought were the conditions under which life was born. Their experiment involved sealing water, methane, ammonia and hydrogen in a sterile flask. The flask was heated to induce evaporation, and then electric sparks were shot through the concoction to simulate lightning strikes. The results were incredible – after a week, five amino acids (the building blocks of life) were found.

But there's one slight issue with the Miller-Urey hypothesis: their soup was wrong. Fossil records from 3.5–4 billion years ago now seem to show that the gases in their flask were almost certainly not present back then. And the flask itself was probably altering the results. So, time for a new idea.

Two decades after Urey and Miller, a team of scientists took a submarine to the deep ocean to study hydrothermal vents, where geothermally heated water gushes through an opening in the seabed. Astonishingly, in these most inhospitable conditions there was life – entire ecosystems, in fact. Today, we call the inhabitants of these places 'extremophiles' thanks to their tolerance of extreme environments.

Why's this important? Well, this discovery changed how we understand the origins of life. It had always been assumed that there were certain necessary conditions, all lying within a fairly narrow band. These extremophiles massively broadened this band. We've found life in extremely hot, cold, acidic and alkaline locations. There's even one microbe, named 'Conan the Bacterium', that can withstand huge doses of radiation.

This has given weight to a theory, proposed by Michael Russell in the late 1980s, that these powerful hydrothermal vents provided both the energy and gases required for life. For instance, an organism might have emerged that could combine the oxygen in the water with hydrogen sulphide from the vents, thereby becoming able to make sugars – the energy of life.

We still don't completely understand how life emerged, or what conditions were necessary for the first step on that DNA ladder (see Genetics, page 28). But just thinking about it is humbling and wondrous. There were once just chemicals and reactions; then, in one universe-changing moment, a nucleic acid (probably RNA) came into being. And billions of years later, here you are, reading this book.

The Circulatory System
Two Billion Beats

Put your finger on your pulse. Feel the thrum-thrum-thrum of your blood pounding around your body and appreciate just how incredible your circulatory system is. Every day, your heart could fill a 2000-litre tanker full of blood. This blood is travelling around your arteries at such great pressure that were we to cut one open right now it would shoot blood up to 5 metres away. Your heart will beat 2 billion times over your lifetime. Your life can be measured as a beating tick to zero.

Blood is an essential, visceral way of understanding being human.

For even the earliest humans, it was obvious that blood *pulses* through your body. Not only can you feel it in your wrist or neck, but if you stab someone deeply enough (and history is full of deep stabbings) your victim's blood leaks out with a pulse. But, until relatively recently, there were some pretty wild theories bandied about.

The first mention of a circulatory system is in ancient Chinese medicine (see page 94). Here, circulation is said to be caused not by some muscular pump but rather by cosmic forces – namely, yin and yang. The three-millennia-old

Indian system of medicine – Ayurveda – argued that when food is digested it's *made* into blood by the liver – suspiciously similar to something Hippocrates 'discovered' in the fourth century BCE. Hippocrates also argued that the purpose of the heart is to cool the blood with air from the lungs (it would be many centuries before air would be seen in terms of oxygen – see page 42 – and carbon dioxide).

William Harvey in the early seventeenth century is usually credited with giving us the first convincing picture of the circulatory system. But, as always, Harvey was standing on the shoulders of giants. Before him, one Greek, one Roman: Aristotle had showed that the heart is the body's central organ, connected (somehow) to all other organs; and Galen knew that arteries contained blood and not air (though he also thought blood was made and then used by the body – not circulated – which would have meant a *vast* production requirement). Vaghbata, who co-wrote the Ayurveda in the seventh century, observed that blood vessels branch outwards, getting ever narrower. And, in the thirteenth century, Ibn al-Nafis suggested that the pulmonary (vein) system ran differently to the main ('systemic') system.

But it was Harvey who put together the whole puzzle. Essentially, the heart pumps out oxygen- and nutrient-rich blood around the body, even to your furthest extremities. Then, the pulmonary system brings oxygen-poor, carbon dioxide-rich blood back up to your heart to be pumped back to the lungs (a process called haematosis).

Learning the mechanics of the circulatory system can feel peculiar. For one, it makes many of us feel squeamish to think of litres of blood pulsing around. But also, in the same way that René Descartes was mocked for his mechanical view of the body, thinking of the heart as a muscle seems ... reductionist somehow. It feels cold-hearted. Yet it is the very stuff of life.

The Nervous System
A Robot of Nerves

Imagine there's a huge, talented and eager orchestra waiting to play, with the usual buzz of restless musicians clutching their horns, waxing their woodwork and twiddling their strings. Let us suppose that this orchestra were told to just *play*. There's no guidance and no instruction at all. What you would get is a terrible, dissonant cacophony. No matter how skilled or brilliant the individual musicians might be, without a conductor our orchestra collapses into a racket.

Our bodies are no different. Without a brain to orchestrate how things work, things get very messy very quickly.

Let's take a moment to appreciate a simpler life – the life of a unicellular organism. They do not have to reflect on things or plan for the future. They do not have to process and navigate the complicated world – they just *are*.

We, though, cursed as we are with a nervous system, must adapt and respond to things. We receive stimuli through our receptor cells (like in the eye or fingers) and have to react appropriately with our effector cells (like muscles or glands). If some trice-cooked chips, slathered in cheese and BBQ sauce, are wafted under your nose, then your salivary glands flood your mouth. Stimuli and response, cause and effect – oh, the misery of a nervous system.

Unsurprisingly, given that we still don't have a complete understanding of the nervous system, history is full of hefty guesswork. Aristotle, following the Egyptians and unfamiliar with dissection (the Greeks thought it taboo), believed the heart controlled all motion and sensation. But Galen – a Roman and not afraid of cutting things open – corrected him by isolating the brain as the seat of all agency (although there are interesting studies recently showing that the gut, for instance, might also have an agency of its own). Galen thought our nerves were like long tubes, through which ran our *spiritus* – the vitality of all life. Ibn Sina gave us the idea of nerves as 'simple membranes'. He sketched various anatomical diagrams, mostly hypothesising about where all these nerves lived. In his hypothesis, we see the beginning of neuroscience.

And it's in this *mechanical* account of the human body that 'the nervous system' takes its place in this book. When Renaissance figures like René Descartes, William Harvey (see page 17) and Leonardo da Vinci started describing the human body as little different to an automaton, it had huge implications for how we saw ourselves. Galen's 'spiritus' – mystical, religious and *special* – was replaced by much more prosaic and humbling physical explanations.

In an age of circuit boards and electrical networks, it's hard not to make comparisons with the human body; the more we develop AI, and the more we understand the nervous system, it looks increasingly like we are just biological machines. After all, if everything we do is simply the effect of a relay down a nervous system, how do we really differ from robots?

Cellular Theory
The Smallest Life Can Get

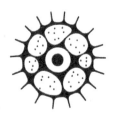

History is written by the winners, and the history of science is no different. When you read about the development of certain scientific ideas, you mostly only hear about the people who turned out to be right. It's called 'hindsight bias' – the inclination to see things as predictable in hindsight. When we say Democritus predicted the atom, the Vedas foresaw heliocentrism or Thales of Timaeus predicted cellular theory, we're being disingenuous. Among the great splat of speculation that thinkers have thrown at the wall, some of it was bound to stick.

In the case of 'cells in the body', we can definitely find early fumblings towards understanding which aren't ridiculous. The ancient Greeks, for instance, commonly thought life meant having some basic blocks, animated by a kind of vital force. But it was all toga-clad guesswork until the invention of the microscope. When Robert Hooke published his 1665 book *Micrographia*, he gave the scientific world its first glimpse into the tiny, invisible parts that make up life. It's a stunningly visual book – depicting crystals, insect anatomy and plant tissue – and it's revelatory, even by today's standards. It's hard to imagine what it must have been like to open it at the time. It's as if someone today were to reveal to us all the fairies and poltergeists that live around us.

One of Hooke's biggest discoveries was the 'cell' (named because it reminded him of a monk's sleeping chamber – the cellula). But he didn't do much with the observation. It's peculiar, in fact, that it took the best part of 200 years to develop what is known as cellular theory. It wasn't until the nineteenth century that the Germans Theodor Schwann and Mathias Schleiden presented two huge facts: cells are the basic building blocks of living things and cells emerge from the division of pre-existing cells.

Today, we know that the cell is the smallest unit of all organisms and it is able to function autonomously. It has two key parts: a nucleus and a gel-like cytoplasm. The nucleus contains DNA and is responsible for cell growth, cell function and mitosis (division). Cytoplasm contains all the 'organelles' which serve all the functioning needs of a cell – not least the mitochondria, which is, as anyone who has ever studied biology knows, the 'powerhouse' of the cell. If the nucleus is the architect, the cytoplasm is the engineer. Or the boss and the employees, the shepherd and the sheep, the general and the army. You get the idea.

You are made up of around 100 billion cells. While each of these are tailor-made to serve the greater purpose (of you), it's also true that they are self-sufficient entities. In some ways, your body is just a confederation of loyal subjects (or a brutal tyranny forcing cells to work way beyond their cellular rights, depending on how you look at it). You are a conglomeration.

The Classification of Life
Putting Things into Boxes

You are, I assume, a mammal (well done, if not!). You might have a canine in your house, or a rodent. Outside, you'll see birds and invertebrates. Your hands are swarming with bacteria (see page 102). All the life around us is neatly categorised. Each living thing is placed in its box, and each box has a big taxonomical label telling you what it means.

It's all thanks to the Swedish son of an amateur gardener, Carl Linnaeus.

Before the eighteenth century, things were classified pretty much according to local custom. Aristotle had tried his best to establish universal rules, and John Ray had formalised an idea of 'species', but at the time Linnaeus went to university, biological taxonomy was a wild west. Names were ridiculous – a linguistic mess of long descriptions, local variations and esoteric flourishes. You might enjoy eating hake, but it would be best to know the regional menus if you wanted to order it. Hake could be Cornish salmon, herring hake or *colin* (if you were French). Some order was needed, and so: Linnaeus.

From an early age, Carl was big on his botany. He and his father would spend hours in the garden, poking, scrutinising and labelling everything. At school, he hated pretty much all of his subjects except Latin, because he knew it would help him to classify his plants. Young Linnaeus was so neglectful of his studies that he was very nearly apprenticed as a cobbler. But it took one teacher – Dr Rothman – to see the potential in the curious, green-fingered boy. Linnaeus lived with Rothman, who taught him for free. In Rothman's accounts, we can see the young Linnaeus already had his own ideas for classification.

The Dean of Uppsala University, Celsius (of temperature fame), saw something brilliant in Carl's ideas, and it was at Uppsala that Linnaeus was encouraged to write his thesis on botanical classification. In it, Linnaeus gave us the system we still use today: *genus + species.* And it cleared things up immensely.

The common briar rose could be called (in Latin) either 'wild rose, white with blush and glabrous leaf' or 'odorous and dog-like white rose'. Linnaeus settled for just 'dog rose'. It really is arbitrary that we accept *Homo sapiens* ('wise man') rather than something like 'featherless biped with propensity for war and beauty'. But Linnaeus made talking about the world much more precise.

What we often take for granted about the classification of life, however, is just how far it conditions our perception of reality. Imagine a world where we did things differently – say we divided by size, by smell or by genome. Ultimately, the Linnaean system is just one way of seeing things, but it is now the only way. It's slightly mind-blowing to think that all living things are defined according to the inclination of a boy who liked gardening with his dad.

Darwinism
Gotta Stay Fit

Imagine a time when so much was unexplained. When people had no idea how the sun rose or set, so the idea of a charioteer racing it across the sky was a reasonable guess. Or imagine not knowing how diseases spread, so the idea of attributing them to malignant celestial alignments sounded actually quite plausible.

But one of the hardest mindsets to envisage is what we believed before Darwin. Think how different your worldview would be if you didn't know that humans were descended from animals. And imagine how cataclysmic this idea must have been when it first appeared. What, after Darwin, did it mean to be human? All sense of being unique, of being special, was suddenly stripped away.

The nineteenth century was still a period of near-universal religious belief, where people turned to priests to answer life's big questions. For instance, many otherwise intelligent people accepted Ussher's calculation that God made the universe in six busy days in October, 4004 BCE. The dinosaurs must've been mighty bored waiting for the rest of Creation to join them.

But then there was Charles Darwin. During a five-year zoological cruise aboard the *Beagle*, he met a British official in the Galápagos who said he could tell exactly which island a tortoise came from, just by the look of its shell. This observation aligned with Darwin's own on finches, and it got him thinking ... for twenty years. This period, known as 'Darwin's delay', ended after a young rival called Wallace looked to release a theory identical to his. By 1859, Darwin finally realised: it was time to publish!

On the Origin of Species was a hot success, selling its entire stock even before publication. The best way to explain its central thesis is by the term 'survival of the fittest'. If an organism is lucky enough to mutate with advantageous traits, it will have 'a better chance of surviving'. The fittest live long enough to pass on their genes; the slow or weak die before they get the chance.

This doesn't mean any one trait is 'better' than another, just that whatever is fittest in a particular environment becomes the dominant trait. It might be sharp talons and huge teeth, or it might be slime and a tiny appetite.

It's thought, today, that evolution is not proven by Darwin's arguments alone. It needed Mendel's work on peas to give us the idea of genes and inheritance, and then Franklin, Watson and Crick to discover DNA (see page 29), before we could say Darwin was right.

So, what does it mean to be a human, now? We're the end product of several millennia of lucky mutations and lots of sex. Darwin's ideas would one day show that we're separated from animals only by lines of DNA, and this humbling fact has revolutionised biology. It's also put us firmly in our place: we're not made in the image of God, we're just large-headed primates who decided to climb down from trees.

Pathology and Germ Theory
Funky Smells and Tiny Microbes

When you read any history of medicine (this book being no less guilty), it's only a matter of time before our modern germ theory is compared with the superstitious nonsense of bygone ages. And, of course, there *was* a lot of superstitious nonsense – divine punishments for lewd thoughts or curses by old women. But a lot of the early medical science people actually used wasn't *that* far removed from the truth.

For a long time, we've known it's not nice to live in a swamp. Not only is there the never-ending torture of mosquitos, but it's also obvious that you're more likely to get a great number of diseases. Most human societies could see this (or something like this) and 'miasma theory' is the best explanation they came up with. Miasma – or 'bad air' – theory is the idea that foul water or air contained invisible, unknown poisonous agents. That's not laughably wrong, is it? In fact, the Roman scholar Varro believed in 'certain minute creatures which cannot be seen by the eyes, which float in the air and enter the body through the mouth and nose and there cause serious diseases'. Which is, basically, how I'd describe germ theory to a child today.

We know now, of course, that germs do not smell, and they do not solely live in fetid air or water. Instead, we know they are the tiny bacteria and viruses that live on pretty much everything. But in order to know that for sure, we needed one thing: the microscope.

It's a politically sensitive decision to single out one person as the 'discoverer' of germ theory in the nineteenth century. It could be Louis Pasteur, Joseph Lister or Robert Koch, depending on which flag you like to wave. Pasteur and Koch hated each other. They criticised and mocked each other through the medium of medical journals (and there is no more vicious forum in human history). While Pasteur was likely the first to present the idea that diseases were caused by foreign organisms, at the risk of offending the French it was the German, Koch, who identified *specific* microorganisms as causing disease.

After Koch's wife, Emmy, fortuitously gifted him a microscope for his birthday, he observed, and grew, a biological arsenal's worth of anthrax bacteria. Years later, Koch also found the tuberculosis bacterium, a germ that is much harder to colour (for microscopes) and much easier to miss than anthrax. After Koch, germ theory was pretty much established – it was only a matter of finding *which* germs caused which diseases, rather than *if* they did.

Today, we wash our hands and take antibiotics (see page 114). We sanitise our water (see page 44) and sterilise medical equipment. Germ theory has made the world a much safer place and it's made people much more involved in their own wellbeing. And we've all got Emmy to thank for her choice of birthday present.

Genetics
You're Pretty Acidic

You share roughly half your genes with a banana, 85 per cent with a guinea pig, and you are statistically identical to all other humans (with a bit of rounding up). If we imagine the human genome as being 260,000 pages, then only 500 pages would be uniquely you. That means that everything you call uniquely 'you' comes from 0.1 per cent of your genes – your eye colour, brain composition, fitness levels, how bad your hangovers are and so on … But percentages hide a lot. Even 0.1 per cent of our individual genomes make up *3 million* base pairs of genes. That's a *lot* of ways to make a human.

With the benefit of hindsight, the earliest science of genetics seems bizarrely ill thought-out. For instance, Aristotle and Pythagoras argued for 'preformation', the idea that a tiny, fully formed human is given by the male sperm, to be grown by the woman's menstrual blood. This was the dominant view up until the seventeenth century. So, for *2,000 years*, people believed humans began as minuscule homunculi that would grow like those horrible sponge toys.

Then, in the 1800s, a monk called Gregor Mendel started growing pea plants. Before Mendel, it was thought that heredity was a bit like a liquid – one parent was Ribena, and the other orange juice, and the result was a russety soup.

Mendel isolated specific attributes of his peas (e.g., crinkliness) and noticed that the offspring was not a mingled compromise but rather inherited the dominant traits of either parent. The world kind of ignored Mendel for half a century (not least because no one cared about peas). Then, in the 1900s, he was rediscovered by William Bateson, who championed Mendel against the sceptics. Bateson coined the term 'genetics', and a new science was born.

The story of genetics is too large to easily summarise here. Names like Thomas Hunt Morgan, George Beadle, Edward Tatum, Oswald Avery, Colin MacLeod and Maclyn McCarty all added their part of the tale, but one of the most famous (and important) contributions was that of James Watson, Francis Crick and Rosalind Franklin. The standard story used to have it that Watson and Crick singlehandedly stumbled on the structure of DNA thanks to their Cambridge-educated genius. The problem with this account is that Watson and Crick's first model wasn't quite right. It was Franklin's X-ray diffraction work (not, at the time, fully acknowledged) that put the Cantabrigians on the right track. This is in no way to downplay their subsequent brilliant work on the double-helix model. Watson has since recognised Franklin's achievement, but sadly she died four years before Watson and Crick won the 1962 Nobel Prize.

DNA is the new frontier of biology (not least because of CRISPR – see page 34). Genetics has given us genetic fingerprinting, crime-scene swabs, GM crops and 'Ancestry DNA' kits for Christmas. DNA is the blueprint of who you are: unravelling that unravels your life.

The Mycelial Revolution
Helpful 'Shrooms

Don't believe the canine propaganda. Dogs are not 'man's best friend'. They're cute, no doubt, but in terms of their contribution to humans? Not a chance. Man's best friend is actually yeast. It's what gives us beer, spirits, bread and cheese. These microorganic pals have been helping to feed humanity – and get us drunk – for millennia.

Yeast is a fungus, and it likes sugar. If you give it a good supply, it'll go at it so happily that not only does it reproduce by the millions but it also gives out two very useful 'waste' products: carbon dioxide and alcohol. So, if you introduce airborne yeast to some fruit and wait a while, what you'll get is a pretty horrible but slightly alcoholic juice. If you leave some fresh orange juice out for a few hours, it'll have around 0.5 per cent alcohol.

More important, though, is how yeast can make leavened bread. Early people would have known about unleavened flatbreads for a long time – mix flour with water and warm it up. Hey presto! Pitta. But if you leave your dough out for a while, then the natural yeasts in certain climates will dive in, digest the sugars in the flour and aerate the dough with their carbonated wind. Finding their dough suddenly three times the size it was earlier that morning, some primitive baker probably just shrugged and threw it in the oven anyway. Today, the 'sourdough starters' that people use in gourmet breads are just a certain species of airborne yeasts. Families or villages would have their own unique yeasty starter, tinkering with it to get the best blend.

So, not only have humans been domesticating cows and horses for several millennia, we've been cultivating microorganisms, too. For most of this time, yeast has been the only fungus of note. That's all set to change in what's billed as the Mycelial Revolution.

When a mushroom takes root, it sends out a small strand known as a hypha. When these hyphae meet with each other, they'll often join forces, form a web and explore outwards. These webs can weave hundreds of miles around forests and they have untold benefits. They give water, minerals and sugars to tree roots – making mycelial forests bigger and stronger than those without. They aerate the soil and make it much more hospitable to all manner of animals.

Scientists, today, are looking at these mycelial webs and thinking, 'They could make stuff for us too.' In fact, it's thought that if we built structures out of mycelium, all we'd need to do is water them and they'd self-repair. Styrofoam and other highly polluting plastics (see page 56) could be replaced by fungi shoots. Mycelium could make clothes, meat-like food, even the scaffolding for organs.

Micro-fungi have been by our side for a very long time. It seems they might help us for a while longer yet.

The Magic of a Tree
The Forgotten Woodland

There's a short story by Roald Dahl called 'The Sound Machine'. It involves a man who invents a machine that allows him to tune into the frequency of surrounding plant life. When he first tries it, he hears the shrieking of roses as his neighbour trims them. Then he hears the soft, low moan of a tree being cut with an axe. Traumatised, he destroys his machine.

This story might not be as far-fetched as we think.

A lot of recent research shows that trees are highly sociable organisms. They have short, hair-like tips at their roots which combine with tiny fungi, enabling them to communicate with one another (see page 31). These root tips act like a kind of awareness for the trees, and they use them to detect if a neighbouring tree is of the same species or if it's a sapling or not. Trees are constantly checking what's going on around them.

And this isn't for nothing. Trees will support one another. If a nearby tree is sick or dying, other trees will feed it sugar solution and nutrients. There have even been cases of 'relationships' amongst trees, where their roots become so enmeshed that they share all their nutrients. Poignantly, if one partner tree dies, the other will not be far behind.

More surprising still, trees have been shown to not only have 'memories' of a sort but to be able to pass these on to their young. Certain apple trees, for instance, will bloom only after 'counting' a certain number of suitably warm days. If they had no sense of memory, they'd have to start the count afresh every day. What's more, if a tree has suffered from a particularly harsh drought, it will adapt its water consumption habits. These habits are then, somehow, passed onto saplings through the soil.

But this is all about forests, and primeval, untouched forests especially. For most of us, our everyday interactions are with the trees dotted along a pavement or lining a park. What do urban conditions do to trees?

Firstly, the trees we see in our cities and towns are often distantly spaced and are made up of a variety of species. This leads to attractive and colourful scenes, but it means that all the benefits of sociability are removed. These trees are denied a support network. They have no parents to nurture and teach them.

Secondly, streetlights interfere with the tree's natural cycles. It might sound odd, but trees actually have a form of 'sleep' during the night-time: their branches sag slightly and water density increases in the trunk and roots. Artificial light distorts this natural rhythm.

Humans have lived alongside trees since the very beginning – we even climbed down *from* those trees. Anyone who's spent time in a deep forest or alone on a canopied walk can attest to their magic. It's a magic we'd be sad to see gone.

CRISPR
The Future of DNA

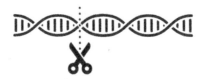

It's 1987, and Yoshi Ishino is in his lab, frowning over some *E. coli*. He's noticed a genetic oddity – the genes of this *E. coli* microbe have a series of five identical DNA segments in a row. Logically possible; statistically improbable. Sadly, genetic science wasn't up to much in the 1980s, so Ishino didn't know what to do with his observation. Fifteen years later, though, some Dutch scientists did. Francisco Mojica and Ruud Jansen renamed these patterns CRISPR – 'clustered regularly interspaced short palindromic repeats' (no wonder we stick with the abbreviation). More importantly, though, Mojica, Jansen, *et al.* noticed something truly incredible: these genes (or, technically, their Cas9 enzymes) could *cut DNA*. They could bind to DNA strands, hop along to whatever bit they wanted and break them up. Imagine highlighting and cutting a wad of text on your word processor. This is what CRISPR was doing – the scissors of the genetic world.

But that was only the start of the mystery.

Evolution doesn't do redundancy, and so pointless, decorative flourishes are usually weeded out. *Why*, then, do these genes cut and potentially edit DNA? What evolutionary reason is there? In 2008, Eugene Koonin noticed that

CRISPR genes – this regular, repeating pattern of genetic letters – looked strikingly similar to viruses. Koonin hypothesised that bacteria were *using* CRISPR to cut genetic lines from the DNA of a virus and paste it into their own 'immune system's' genome. They were, essentially, making their own vaccinations (see page 100).

As with many entries in this book, the implications of this discovery were lost for a good while. For five years, the most revolutionary idea in biology this century was deployed to make bacteria-resistant yoghurts, giving them a slightly longer shelf life. It took an American biochemist and French microbiologist, Jennifer Doudna and Emmanuelle Charpentier, to untap the huge potential CRISPR had to offer (winning them Nobel Prizes in the process).

To understand how CRISPR does its thing, we need first to know that it not only cuts and copies virus DNA (as a kind of vaccination) but then it uses this knowledge to destroy future appearances of that virus. It's like CRISPR is a police chief who puts up a 'Most Wanted' poster in Immune System Command. When that virus appears, the immune system police know to take it down. What Doudna and Charpentier realised was that if they could make their own 'Most Wanted' poster, CRISPR would hunt for and snip out that sequence of DNA.

CRISPR has opened up a huge and hopeful but largely as-yet-unknown frontier. It's transforming agriculture, curing diseases and possibly bringing back the woolly mammoth. But it's also got a darker side. It makes real the possibility of designer babies and human mutants. If there's one thing this book shows, it's naïve to think a technology remains good and pure for long.

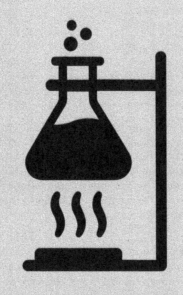

Chemistry

Chemistry is sometimes called the 'central science' because it lies at the nexus between mathematics, physics, biology, medicine, geology and environmental studies. It's all about the reactions and properties of substances, and how chemicals behave. It's chemistry that tells us which drugs will cure a disease, what fuel will give off the most energy and which powder will make the prettiest firework.

Chemistry is about not only how chemicals work but how they can be applied to our lives.

Alchemy
Get Rich Quick

There's nothing new about 'get rich quick' schemes. In the course of human history, if ever there were the prospect of an effortless way of getting minted, you can guarantee someone will have tried it. For much of the past, this meant alchemy. Alchemy is about trying to turn one chemical into another (mostly gold), but it's also a worldview and philosophy – a quasi-religion with its own disciples and heresies.

Alchemy has always lived in the borderlands between science and the mystical. Consider Daoism (see page 286). Today this is often thought to be about yin-yang, tai chi and enigmatic riddles. But, as it was *practised* across history, it involved a great conical flask's-worth of alchemy. Daoists were constantly on the lookout for the 'elixir of life' – the potion of immortality, also known as the 'philosopher's stone'. It's an alchemical pursuit mirrored across many cultures.

For Isaac Newton, alchemy represented a mystery. In the 1660s, he had a huge, multi-year sulk at the scientific community for criticising his work, and spent the years obsessively trying to unravel the mysteries of alchemy. Given the practice was made illegal not long before Newton's birth, this secretive, cloistered research was never published.

Most of us understand 'alchemy' as the quasi- or proto-scientific attempt to transmute one element into another. In the natural world, materials often seem to transform: iron rusts, copper turns green and salt dissolves in water. So, it makes sense to assume that we could artificially convert one metal or mineral into another. Some of the greatest scientists in history – Paracelsus, Jābir ibn Ḥayyān, Roger Bacon – were all fixated on alchemy. They used powders to blow things up and acids to dissolve them; they froze liquids and they burned solids; they buried lead in excrement and submerged iron in blood. All to no avail. For alchemists, as with a lot of pseudoscientists, the answer was always just around the corner – they just needed a new, elusive elixir.

Not all of this was time wasted, however. Alchemists were the early chemists who developed the scientific method and, although misguided in their objectives, discovered a great many things along the way. They gave us distillation (so you have them to thank for your whisky), gold plating and urine analysis (which, up to that point, involved tasting and smelling alone). Alchemy gave us things like zinc, phosphorus, arsenic and gunpowder.

Today, we know that turning one element into another is impossible (at least without a nuclear reaction). With our periodic tables (see page 46) and modern physics, we see alchemists as either naïve or charlatans. In fact, that view was taken even at the time. Conmen, religious fanatics and snake-oil peddlers would often try to get people to part with their money and invest in alchemy. As an eighteenth-century expression handed down to us goes: 'There's no alchemy like saving.'

The Conservation of Matter
You're Not Going Anywhere

We cannot be destroyed. No matter how hard my wife might try, there's nothing that can get rid of me. You and I are here for forever ... but probably not in the way we would like. It's all to do with the conservation of matter. This is the idea that you cannot destroy or create matter, you can only change its arrangement. All life is simply an exchange of energy. The entire universe is just particles in different configurations. The bits that now make up your hands or your brain will never 'die'. They'll float away as ashes in the wind. We never 'disappear', we just become worm food.

Let's go back to pre-Revolution France. It's 1774, and in a laboratory, wearing his finest tight-fitting trousers and goat's-hair wig, sits Antoine Lavoisier. He's burning things in a glass. Lavoisier is trying to isolate that peculiar thing we now know is oxygen (see page 42) but what he notices as he experiments is just as monumental. As he heats tin inside a closed vessel, he sees that the metal first burns, then smokes, then solidifies again. The odd thing is that at no time does the mass of the entire glass change.

Then, as now, it's a pretty counterintuitive idea. To those of a non-scientific mindset, gases have no weight at all. It's assumed that invisible means absent. Yet what Lavoisier showed is that in a closed environment, mass never changes. If I were to hermetically seal you into a room, then five million years later, the room and its contents would weigh the same (although you might look a bit worse for it). Of course, we do not live in a vacuum, so we breathe, sweat and excrete all the time. When you walk into someone's house, you're just donating mass to them (unless, of course, you eat their biscuits – then it goes both ways).

It's this vision of the universe – as atomic mass temporarily encased in this or that object – that informs how we understand 'states of matter'. Everything around you now is either a solid, liquid, gas or plasma (which, for the purposes of this book, can be treated as 'energy'). The difference between them is simply how densely packed their particles are.

For a lot of things, heat acts as the 'transition stage' – add enough heat and you spread out the particles; chocolate (yum) turns to chocolatey goo (yummier!) which turns to chocolatey vapour (okay, too far). But there are also a great many things that skip the liquid stage, going straight from solid to gas at high temperature, which is called 'sublimation'.

So, enjoy the temporary configuration of particles that you call 'me'. One day, when those particles pull apart, you'll rejoin the universe. You might become a beautiful shooting star, a morning dew drop or a spring flower. Or, or course, you might just become a cow turd.

Oxygen

Explosive and Breathable

We're so used to our current way of thinking that it's sometimes hard to imagine the scientific worldview of the past. Try to believe, now, that your liver is constantly making blood or that the world is made up only of the four 'classical elements' (earth, wind, water and fire). One of the more resilient theories was the idea that when something burned it gave off a special substance called 'phlogiston'. All reactions were thought to be an exchange of this phlogiston, and an excess of the stuff polluted the air around us, making it stale and dangerous.

It was against this intellectual background that two of the greatest chemists in history take their bow: Joseph Priestley (1733–1804) and Antoine Lavoisier (1743–1794).

Priestley was not born to academia – he was one of six children and his father was a clothier. He was banned from formal university study because of his family's unorthodox religious beliefs. But great minds can rarely be kept still. Living next door to a brewery in Leeds, he noticed that the gas emitted from the vats would extinguish flames. With nothing but a bit of gumption and a home chemistry kit, he studied carbon dioxide (not yet named that, of course). He went on to find fame from selling fizzy water, after which his friends and patrons encouraged him to formally take up chemistry.

It was Priestley who first offered the idea that 'dephlogisticated air' – what we now call oxygen – was a necessary condition for living things, since mice were more active (that is to say, more alive) if they were entrapped in it. It's also what allows fires to burn. Of course, dephlogisticated air is not quite right. Priestley's inability to see past the science of his day made him miss one big thing. For that, we need to meet Lavoisier.

Lavoisier was the chalk to Priestley's cheese. Rich, educated and with the best of French chemistry at his disposal, it was Lavoisier who discovered it wasn't that phlogiston made the air stale but rather that a gas (which he called 'oxygen') was necessary to make it breathable. He proved the existence of oxygen by burning phosphorus in a bell jar (not, this time, a closed jar – see page 40), noting that the mass of the phosphorus *after* combustion was heavier than the original sample. So, he theorised, oxygen was passing from the air to the phosphorus. He was quite right.

Schooled as we are with periodic tables and that infuriating element song (YouTube it, you'll not thank me later), we take the revolutionary idea of elemental gases for granted. There's nothing obvious in the world to suggest the existence of hydrogen, oxygen, nitrogen and so on. To be able to not only postulate the idea but to *prove* it was quite remarkable. It's seeing the invisible and making the unknown known. The story of oxygen illustrates the genius of eighteenth-century science.

Water Purification
Wells and Wellness

It's a modern miracle that, waking up thirsty at 3 a.m., bleary-eyed and semi-conscious, you can turn on a tap and get fresh, clean and deliciously cold water. Water that is nourishing and healthy. Water that you can drink, cook with and bathe in. It's an engineering and scientific marvel that, running beneath your feet one way, there passes water that is refreshing and safe. The other way there runs water which is fetid and rank. Pre-modernity, that was an unthinkable luxury.

There are essentially two kinds of water purification: clarification and bacterial reduction. Clarification means removing all the horrid muck to leave only water. Since ancient times, people have used various filtering techniques, such as simply passing water through woven fabric to take out the grit. And it's hard not to notice that if you leave a liquid long enough, the heavy bits drop to the bottom (sedimentation), leaving water on top. This gave the Romans a good idea: 'settling reservoirs', where muddy or churned water was kept in an artificial lake for a period of time to settle, before aqueducts funnelled the water to a city's inhabitants. Of course, if it rained or if the winds picked up, the water was still mucky. This is why many aqueducts would also have grills or grates to catch the worst of the muck.

But we know, today, that muddy water does not necessarily mean dangerous water and that clear water isn't always safe. Before the last few centuries, people had no idea about bacteria carried in water, and so 'purification' simply meant using mechanical or chemical techniques to make water *look* or taste nice. The ancient Greek armies did notice that their troops would get ill less often when they boiled their water (when there were no fresh water sources nearby), but they didn't know why.

The story of 'why' goes back to John Snow in Victorian England. In 1854, London was in the diarrheal clutches of a cholera epidemic. The leading physicians of the day thought it was all to do with foul air and airborne pathogens (see page 26). Snow, though, suspected germs within the water. He drew overlapping maps of outbreak hotspots and noticed they triangulated around certain water sources – one of which was the famous Broad Street Well. When the pump handle was removed from the well (preventing the drawing of water), the number of cholera cases fell away. Snow might not have *proved* the existence of water-borne pathogens but he made it statistically and epidemiologically incontrovertible.

Today, we know Snow was right, and we add chemicals like chlorine to rid water of bacteria and other nasties. Water treatment plants will often use UV light to do the job, chemical-free. Which is a good thing, because at 3 a.m., bleary-eyed and semi-conscious, who wants to boil and filter their water?

The Periodic Table

The Universe in Rows

A great many wonderful things have been 'discovered' in a dream. Mary Shelley had a nightmarish vision of *Frankenstein*, Paul McCartney dreamt up the melody to 'Let It Be' and Larry Page got the idea for Google. When I dream, I get pigs talking about TV programmes in bad Spanish accents. I feel my unconscious is letting me down. One of the most scientifically important dreams in history came one night in February 1869, when Dimitry Mendeleev was gifted the periodic table. The contents of Mendeleev's unconscious mind are now blazoned across classrooms the world over.

Everything you see around you, right now, is the special combination of the same ninety-two naturally occurring elements. If you imagine the elements to be like letters, then the universe is basically just a huge book. What Mendeleev gave us is the equivalent of the alphabet – a way to systematise and recognise all the elements that make up the water in your shower, the plant on your desk and the toenails on your feet. Having a finite list of elements represented a paradigm shift in our view of the world. Before the chemical elements came along, the fundamental blocks of the universe were the concern of religion, quackery or unhinged metaphysicians.

The periodic table is made up of seven rows. The double row at the bottom is only there to save space – these elements actually belong to rows six and seven. All of the elements from one to ninety-two are naturally occurring on Earth, even if in minuscule quantities. All the elements from ninety-three onwards are artificially made – by things like nuclear reactions, particle accelerators or Dr Strange.

The idea is that, reading the table from left to right, each element has one more proton in its nucleus than the last (this is the atomic number). So, why is it called the 'periodic' table? Well, it's because the horizontal rows are known as periods. (If I were in charge of Mendeleev's PR, I would have gone for 'atomic' table.)

The reason the periodic table is so important to chemists and schoolteachers worldwide is that it allows us to explain why elements behave the way they do and to predict *how* they will behave. So, for example, knowing that sodium and potassium are both located in group one (and so have one valence electron) means we know both are likely to be highly reactive with non-metals, making them popular in industrial processes. This knowledge opens the possibility of creating even more elements – which sounds like either an exciting, hopeful future or the dastardly plot of a sci-fi villain, depending on your perspective.

Many of us will have horrible, Pavlovian associations with the periodic table. It reminds us of dusty school laboratories, teachers' droning voices and Chloe Reddish getting all the answers right. But, with age, we can see it in a new light – as a map to the universe … or, if you're so inclined, as God's workstation.

Explosives
Better Ways to Blow Things Up

I'm not one to pedantically rip apart the historical accuracy of movies. I'm firmly of the school of thought that says entertainment should be entertaining and that if a historical fact would make for a dull film, it should be culled. Take the *Pirates of the Caribbean* franchise, for instance. These swashbuckling romps never go long without some huge sea battle or musket duel. Yet if these scenes were accurate, the action would disappear in a haze of blackish, suffocating smoke. At naval battles like Trafalgar, after the first few volleys of shots, impure gunpowder would make the battlefield a blind hellscape of sulfuric mist.

It was this that partially triggered the nineteenth-century explosion of explosives.

It's one of the most famous ironic legacies of history, but Alfred Nobel – who endowed the Nobel *Peace* Prize – made his fortune by making dynamite. By mixing in fossilised algae, Nobel created a much more stable form of the explosive nitroglycerine – otherwise known as TNT – and he also invented a smokeless gunpowder called ballistite. But when Nobel read a

French newspaper calling him 'the merchant of death', he was distraught. So distraught, in fact, that he committed (some) of his fortune to the Peace Prize we still have today.

But, of course, hawkish generals and empire-hungry monarchs saw the huge potential in Nobel's work (it should also be mentioned that Nobel can't have been *that* distraught, given he spent the last half of his life creating more weapons). From the 1870s onwards, gunpowder was near obsolete and newer, better and cheaper forms of explosives were here.

There are, essentially, two types of explosives:

First, there are 'low explosives'. These are chemicals (often called propellants) which are lit by a cap or a primer, then their combustion acts to propel a missile or bullet at some ridiculous speed towards a target. When the likes of Nobel used chemistry to produce cleaner and more efficient explosives, they enabled the speedy propellants needed for quick-firing guns, as well as huge, armour-piercing shells.

Second, there are 'high explosives', which you see on TV when that really old, ugly building you grew up near finally gets demolished. High explosives are intended to detonate; they don't need to *propel* so much as create a seismic shockwave big enough to destroy a lot of concrete. Even today, high explosives are usually a kind of dynamite, using nitroglycerine mixed either with ammonium or gelatine, depending on your destruction needs. Grenades use high explosives, as does *Lethal Weapon 1, 2* and *3*.

Explosives are, obviously, controversial. They have existed for a very long time indeed, in artillery, fireworks and signals as far back as ancient China (see page 210). They are far more often used for ill than for good, and most people probably associate them with artillery or suicide bombers rather than controlled mining explosions. A bit like fire, explosives are a dangerous servant.

The Internal Combustion Engine
Efficiency Is Cool

'Efficiency' is, usually, a bit boring. If someone says they need to 'streamline efficiency', it's hard not to roll your eyes and sigh inwardly. The job of this book is to draw out the more interesting and important developments across human discovery. And so you'll note that I often zip through centuries' worth of science with the words 'various people improved on this' or 'later scientists went on to make it more efficient'. In the process, I've hoped to save you from some of the more soporific aspects of invention.

But, just occasionally, we need to focus on efficiency.

The invention of the steam engine was a huge moment in scientific history (see page 214). It powered the industrialisation of Europe, it fed the hungry mouths of booming new cities, and it catalysed the scientific revolution. But if you've ever actually watched a steam train fire up and get moving ... well, you should probably bring some sandwiches. The steam engine is not very efficient at transferring energy. It is an *external* combustion engine, meaning the heat source comes from outside the propulsion mechanism. A sweaty, begrimed worker shovels coal into a firebox to heat the boiler – a bit like a gas hob under your pot of pasta. The problem is this wastes a *lot* of energy. In the hob example, heat goes up to the pot, yes, but a considerable amount simply wafts out into your kitchen.

Much better, then, if we could somehow get the hob *inside* the pot. That way, all of the energy source can be utilised for streamlined efficiency. Which is what we get with the *internal* combustion engine. The problem, though, is that this is near impossible with inefficient fuels like coal or wood. You need to burn a lot of those to get a good amount of energy, not to mention the fact that both are heavy and space-consuming. So, when Nikolaus Otto invented his four-stroke combustion engine in 1876, he needed a different fuel: petroleum or gasoline. The 'four strokes' of Otto's machine essentially involve mixing air and gasoline on one stroke, building up pressure on another stroke and igniting the cocktail on another. A final stroke gets rid of all the waste – the exhaust stroke. All of which makes a much more powerful piston to move whatever you want moving.

... And people wanted a lot of things moving. In 1885, Carl Benz gave us the first completely self-propelled vehicle – the 'Motorwagen' – with a whopping 0.75 horsepower engine (although with a different engine to Otto's). By the twentieth century, the internal combustion engine allowed Henry Ford's iconic Model T to reach eye-watering speeds of 40–45mph and the Wright brothers to give the world flight (see page 224).

Once again, we see that the story since then is of various people going on to make things much more efficient. And so the march of progress continues ...

Electrons
Let's Get Basic

If you're sitting on a chair right now, you're not actually sitting *on* the chair. In fact, you're hovering just above it due to a magic known as 'Coulombic repulsion'. You and your closest loved ones will never be able to touch. You'll always be kept apart by an electric field. (On the plus side, you also won't be able to put your hand straight through them.) All the atoms in your body have electrons orbiting about their nuclei like tiny planets (although the image of planetary orbiting is not quite right, these days). These electrons have negative charges. All the atoms in your mate Dave's body, in your chair, or that make up the ground – they also have negatively charged electrons. Like two magnets, impossible to join, your body is kept apart from everything there is.

We once thought that atoms were the fundamental building blocks of the universe. In fact, the world 'atom' literally means 'uncuttable'. So, when some Cambridge scientists first split the atom, it was quite the etymological faux pas. We now know that inside an atom is a solar system of activity, made up of electrons, protons, neutrons and quarks. But none of this was known until a scientist named J. J. Thomson (no, not me) came along.

Humans have known about something *like* electricity for a long time – it's seen in electric eels and lightning, for instance. But despite all the research of Faraday and Maxwell (see page 71), we only dealt with the *effects* of electricity and didn't know what caused it. It was J. J. Thomson who proved that electricity was caused not by waves, as many people thought, but by 'charged' *particles*.

Electrons are incomprehensibly small particles that carry a negative charge. Assuming your atom isn't ionised, just enough electrons attach themselves to its nucleus to perfectly balance out the nucleus's positive charge. The magical aspect to this, though, is we don't know *why* this happens. There's no known law or explanation for why electrons have exactly an equal and opposite amount of charge to balance out the positive charge of the nucleus.

Electrons are very, very light, which makes them easy to accelerate and move around. The big advantage to this is that we can fire them at stuff. When we do this, we can see inside the structure of things – like atoms. It's what allows us to use electron microscopes, which produce ridiculously detailed and clear images of ridiculously small things.

The electron is, as far as has been proven, one of the 'basic' units of the universe. Which means it cannot (yet) be broken down further. String theorists (see page 86), however, hypothesise that even these might be made up of tiny, vibrating strings. When Thomson found the electron lurking inside an atom, he proved again that you should never assume one answer is going to be the right one forever.

The Haber-Bosch Process
The Biggest Unknown Idea

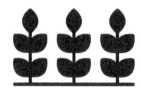

You're likely to be familiar with most of the ideas in this book – the wheel (see page 204), monotheism (page 282) and cell biology (page 20) are all pretty well known. But however big these ideas are, it's unlikely they can match the transformative heft of the Haber-Bosch process. Without it, *half the world* would starve. Yet most people know nothing about it.

All plants need nitrogen to grow but they can't absorb it directly from the air. Instead, plants have to get their nitrogen from the soil or from fertiliser, often in the form of ammonium – hydrogen and nitrogen combined (NH_4+), which is found in animal manure and rotten vegetables. Farmers for millennia had been using bird droppings, slurry, cow dung and so on to give their crops valuable nitrogen. But by the turn of the twentieth century, despite all the straining cows and obliging birds, there just wasn't enough fertiliser to go around. It looked likely that the world population would stagnate for lack of crops.

Enter Fritz Haber. There's a law in chemistry known as Le Châtelier's principle, which states that, for a system in equilibrium, if you change one side of that balance, the system will act to counter the change. Haber used this principle to engineer the making of ammonia. People had known that ammonia would decompose when placed on nickel. What Haber realised was that with the right temperature (roughly 650°C) and high pressure, and with iron as a catalyst, you could make small amounts of ammonia from the hydrogen and nitrogen in the air.

With the help of a chemical factory run by Carl Bosch, the Haber-Bosch process was upsized to pump out huge quantities of fertiliser. Today, roughly half of all food production uses fertiliser made by this process.

But Haber was not some great humanitarian set on solving world hunger. First, the ammonia produced by his discovery was just as useful in explosives (see page 48) as it was for fertiliser. It was whisked away to the munitions factories of the First World War far quicker than to any farmer's field. Second, Haber was so vehemently nationalistic that he turned his genius to developing chemical weapons for Germany. He famously wrote: 'In peace-time the scientist belongs to humanity, in war-time to his fatherland.' An attitude that led directly to the gas shells that landed in Allied trenches all over Europe.

Rarely in life is anyone straightforwardly a hero or villain, and the Haber story is morally grey. Here was a man who gave the world one of the greatest discoveries of all time. But he was also a nationalistic weapons-manufacturer, quite happy to use whatever means possible to kill thousands. Haber's story illustrates that of science more broadly. Used for good, it can better the world beyond imagining. Used for ill, can cause limitless harm.

Polymers
Fake Plastic Trees

If you're a reasonably aware person, I can safely bet you already know plastics are a problem. Plastics pollute our seas, form mountains of unbiodegradable rubbish, and it's thought that roughly five grams of the stuff will pass through your gut this week. We know this is all bad, but we also know just how dependent we are on them. Look around you now. Try to count how many things are made of, or with, plastic. You'll fall asleep before you finish.

Whether we like it or not, we can no longer easily live without plastic. Given it's a relatively recent invention, that's quite a feat.

If I were intelligent enough to invent something useful, I would almost certainly name it after myself. Which is exactly what Alexander Parkes did when he created the first plastic in 1862. Parkes dissolved cotton fibres in some acids, mixed this with vegetable oil and gave us 'Parkesine'. Cruelly for Parkes, the world utterly disregarded his own choice of name and rebadged it celluloid – the first plastic. Celluloid was useful for a few things (billiard balls and combs are probably the first things made with plastic) but it never really went mainstream – although it was used in photography and film for a while. Plastics like Perspex and Bakelite were early twentieth-century improvements, but they had only a few, limited uses.

The Second World War changed things. The various militaries of the world realised how versatile and cheap plastic was. You could have unbreakable bottles, grenades encased in Bakelite (to keep the ignition fumes contained) and plane windscreens that didn't kill you if they cracked. When the war ended, the huge new plastics industry needed to turn its polythene eyes elsewhere. They landed on public consumer goods.

Plastic, nowadays, creeps into every walk of life. It gives us tights, shopping bags, Tupperware, electrical insulation, children's toys (and adult toys), polystyrene foam, acrylic paints, and on and on it goes. Even the flag Neil Armstrong planted on the moon was made of nylon. Given that the plastic bottle is one of the more conspicuous plastic products around today, it's curious that it arrived relatively late to the party. It took until 1973 for manufacturers to develop plastic strong enough (called PET) to withstand the high pressures of carbonation.

Despite all the wastage and environmental damage plastics cause, there's no sign of them going away soon. In fact, the opposite is true: the future is plastic. Plastics are necessary for nanotechnologies, modern aircraft, smart phones, prosthetics, cars and 3D printing. In 2013, the Liberator, the world's first print-at-home plastic gun, was controversially made available online.

So, if we are to tear ourselves away from plastics, we need to find a general-purpose replacement soon (plastic bonds are not found in nature, so no natural species, like bacteria, have evolved to break them down ... yet). If we don't, then graveyard oceans, cities of plastic bags and stomachs full of plastic will be here to stay.

The Pill

The Capsule of Choice

Not everyone wants to have children but most people want to have sex. And herein lies a millennia-old conundrum: how to have fire without smoke? How can you shake the sheets without joining the club? For that, you need contraception. When you look back at the myriad ways people have tried to stop getting pregnant, you can't help but both admire and grimace at human ingenuity. After all, nothing is sexier than a pig-bladder condom; no amorous encounter is complete without a lemon rind cervical cap; and no man is more appealing than when covered in crocodile turds (what the ancient Egyptians used).

The history of contraception is usually the history of accidental babies. Even in the modern era, condoms are only 80 per cent successful (mainly because of neglectful manhandling). Which is why the invention of the contraceptive pill, first developed in 1950s America, changed the world.

Anyone who's spent thirty seconds around a baby knows just how life-overwhelming they can be. If you're a young, hard-working woman still in education, or if you've just started your career, then getting pregnant and having a baby is, for most, a chain-yanking stop.

Yes, we all know women who *do* heroically juggle motherhood with high-flying careers, but for many people around the world this is still a challenge. So, in a pre-contraceptive society, where having sex meant a high chance your life plans would be burnt to the ground, your only options were to abstain or risk it (options that men could ignore, of course). Add to this the social pressure and human *need* to have sex, and the lack of contraceptive options essentially forced women to be low-paid or housebound mothers. No surprise, then, that politics, academia and the workplace were all entirely dominated by men up until the 1970s.

The thing that changed that? The pill. On a biological level, the pill contains the hormones oestrogen and progesterone, and the early variants were designed to prevent ovulation (no egg, no fertilisation). Modern 'combined' pills also do other things, like making it harder for sperm to reach the womb or for a fertilised egg to implant. On a *social* level, the pill gave women choice. It allowed them to take control of their own fertility. They could decide to train as a doctor, a lawyer, a politician, whatever, without the risk it would all be for naught. It empowered women.

No one thing can be solely responsible for this or that revolution. The pill came in tandem with a shift in the zeitgeist, led by activists and feminists like Margaret Sanger, Simone de Beauvoir and Gloria Steinem. But in terms of the power of a single invention to upend the social and economic fabric of our society, there's little in this book to beat the pill.

Physics

There's a widely inaccurate cliché that says philosophy and religion are concerned with the 'why' of the world but science is concerned only with the 'how'. Yet at the heart of physics, and in the minds of all great physicists, is the pressing need to know why things happen. Physics is about the foundations of the universe. It's about the laws, structures and unfathomable behaviours that underpin everything we know.

Studying physics is an attempt to understand the keys to our universe (and all others ...).

Maths
The Digital Metaverse

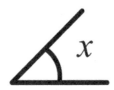

All biology is chemistry, all chemistry is physics, and all physics is maths. Or so say the mathematicians (who will be thrilled, I'm sure, to see their life's passion reduced to a chapter in the Physics section). The entire fabric of the universe – everything there is and ever will be – can be reduced to equations and algorithms. Which is lucky, because humans are great at maths. From our earliest past, as a species we have fallen in love with these abstract representations dancing around on tablets and paper.

Most of us tend to think of maths as some universal practice – as true for cavemen as for modern professors. But that's not strictly accurate. A 'base' in maths is the range of numbers you can use – essentially, how many numerals you have. In our modern (Hindu-Arabic) system, we have a base of ten. We have ten digits from 0 to 9 and then we put them together to make bigger numbers.

Five thousand years ago, though, the Babylonians were using a base of sixty, adopting the system from the Sumerians. Sixty was useful because it divides really well into fractions. The reason we have sixty seconds to a minute and 360 degrees in a circle is because of the Babylonians. Right angles, straight lines and circles are understood easily in base sixty. The ancient Greeks – including Pythagoras, Zeno and Archimedes – built on what went before but greatly expanded their understanding. Euclid formalised the 'axioms' of mathematics, which are the essential, inviolable rules of maths that we need to accept before we go about our business. The way operators work (like addition and subtraction) are axioms, but so too are rules like 'two straight, parallel lines will never meet' (except, possibly, at infinity).

Why, then, do we teach Hindu-Arabic numerals at school? Two reasons, really. The first is that the Arabic world was the successor of the Greek's, when it came to defining maths. The words 'algorithm', 'algebra', 'average' and 'cipher' all owe themselves to Islamic scholars. When Europeans encountered these brilliant ideas, they found it easier to simply reuse Hindu-Arabic numbers. Fibonacci of Italy, for instance, in his book *Liber Abaci*, thought they 'had an eye to usefulness and future convenience'. The second reason is that the Hindu-Arabic system had a concept previously unconsidered (or at least unrepresented): zero. Originally, zero was simply a placeholder in decimal tables for bigger numbers, for instance: 1.0.0.0.2 (10002). But over time the concept of 'nothingness' developed a status of its own.

The ability to think mathematically is one of the most curious and remarkable accomplishments of the human mind. It underpins everything from engineering and architecture to the very laws of nature. It orders the random and brings symmetry to a world that's wobbly. While maths is, in many ways, a made-up language, it is also its own metaphysical universe of numbers and axioms. When we do maths, it's easy to *feel* like we're reaching towards something pure and true.

Heliocentrism

A New, Copernican Way of Seeing Things

It's not at all apparent from our senses alone that the world is made up of atoms, or that diamonds and coal are forms of the same element, or that we have cells containing DNA which codes how our bodies work. Sometimes, science has to rewire how we see the world.

Never is this truer than in the 'Copernican Revolution': the idea that the universe does not, in fact, revolve around our planet.

If you knew nothing of science, it would seem boringly obvious that the sun moves around us. After all, we can watch the sun move through the sky and then park itself out of sight at night. What's more, the ground beneath our feet clearly does not spin. Add to all this the fact that geocentrism (the idea that the Earth is the centre of the universe) was the official position of the Christian Church, and it's no wonder that for many centuries no one thought, or dared, to challenge the idea.

In Nicolaus Copernicus' day, established astronomical wisdom came from the Roman scholar Ptolemy. His geocentric theory survived for 1400 years because it works pretty well for naked-eye observations and is reasonably accurate at predicting planetary movements. If it ain't broke, don't fix it.

Copernicus (1473–1543), though, saw the cracks. As he was reading some Archimedes, Copernicus noticed a throwaway reference to Aristarchus of Samos, who had postulated that the *sun* was the centre of the cosmos (Archimedes himself laughed the idea away). Other scholars in the ancient Islamic and Christian world had also suggested the idea but none had done much about it.

At least part of the reason for the change from geocentrism to heliocentrism was simple practicality. Working out the positions of the planets ahead of time was hugely important to farmers, sailors and explorers. What's more, the Julian calendar (established by Julius Caesar) was playing merry hell with the Church's dates for Easter – they were moving earlier and earlier. So, ironically (given that Galileo was nearly executed for proving Copernicus' theory), the original heliocentric theory was partially an attempt to aid the Church's 'Gregorian' calendar reforms.

But for such a famous moment in the history of science, Copernicus' actual theory is pretty underwhelming. In reality, he didn't do much more than offer an alternative view to the same data available to Ptolemy. And, like his Roman predecessor, he mistakenly thought planets moved in circular orbits (they're actually elliptical) and at uniform speeds.

Copernicus was radical, no doubt, but his genius lay only in his ability to think outside the box. It was Galileo, more than half a century later, who was the first to *prove* heliocentrism, thanks to a nifty little Dutch invention: the telescope.

But the main legacy of Copernicus lies in how revolutionary he was. After a millennium and a half of scientific inertia, he showed that the Church and accepted wisdom, both, were not infallible. Copernicus led the way in reigniting an empirical curiosity about the world.

Newtonian Mechanics
Big People Are Attractive

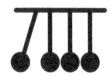

Often in the history of science, you miss the people behind the stories. With Isaac Newton, more needs to be said. Behind the name 'Newton' lies pretty much all classical physics. Although there were a great many other contributors, it's his name which is almost synonymous with macrocosmic physics – we even call it *Newtonian* mechanics.

Newton was born the year Galileo died (1642), and if you're into reincarnation, that might give you pause for thought. Even from his earliest schooldays, it was clear that Newton was a difficult person. He was antisocial and sharp-tongued, and he lived most of his life alone with few friends. He took criticism *very* seriously. When a crook called William Chaloner accused Newton – then overseeing the Royal Mint – of embezzlement, Newton obsessively stopped at nothing to build a case so strong against Chaloner that the latter was eventually hanged.

But, for all his eccentricities, Newton gave us three famous 'laws' and one huge idea: gravity.

First law: *Something will remain still or at a constant speed unless something else acts to prevent it*. Essentially, things do not stop and start on their own.

A marble rolling along a flat surface will eventually stop thanks to friction and air resistance.

Second law: *The greater the force, the greater the acceleration.* If I attach an F1 engine to a supermarket trolley, it will accelerate very quickly. If there's a huge tidal wave, it'll cause lots of damage. If you really want something, you can get it (okay – that one isn't physics).

Third law: *Every action has an equal reaction – the push matches the pull.* Imagine a fish using its tail to swim. The force used to push the fish forwards will be the same as the force that pushes the water it's in backwards.

Gravity, like dark matter/energy (see page 88), was more postulated than discovered. It's necessary for every calculation dealing with space, planets and galaxies to work. It's a 'fundamental force' – if it weren't there, nothing we know about the universe would make sense. Newton showed that gravity is a force of attraction between any objects with mass, with the smaller attracted to the larger at a greater rate than vice versa. So, the moon is gravitationally pulled towards the Earth but is prevented from crashing into it by their mutual orbits. This book is, by a very weak pull, inclined to move towards you. If you're sitting next to someone, then you are gravitationally attracted to each other (with the heavier person accelerating less). Of course, all of this is barely detectable when set against the gravitational big boy in the room: the Earth.

Newton was a genius. A difficult, contrary and prickly genius. His ideas changed not only science but also how we understood the universe. No longer was it the magical, mysterious script of God, but instead a finely tuned, delicately balanced mechanical system.

Wave-Particle Duality
Neither This Nor That

It's a good rule in life not to take anything too seriously. Laughter is, after all, the best medicine, and something ridiculed can rarely be scary. So smile when you can and mock everything. It's a lesson written into the very fabric of existence because, when you learn about quantum mechanics, it's clear that the universe is having us on.

The wave vs. particle debate goes back to the seventeenth century. Isaac Newton (see page 66), the man to beat and the man who did some beating, did extensive work on light – on prisms, refraction, reflection and so on – and, in the main, he was bang on the money. Newton postulated that light was a particle-like ray (what he called a 'corpuscle'). Over in the Netherlands, though, bewigged Christiaan Huygens was having none of it. Huygens was a titan of physics in his own right. He invented the pendulum clock (see page 213), measured Saturn's rings and invented his own, improved, telescope. He was also bold enough to take on Newton. Huygens noticed that light demonstrated certain *wave*-like properties – namely diffraction (when a wave can bend around an object) and interference (where two meeting waves will add together or cancel one another out).

As it happens, Newton and Huygens respected each other hugely. The problem is that being a wave or a particle is mutually exclusive, and yet both make sense, in some contexts. Three hundred years later, we're not much closer to the answer; quantum physics just can't make its mind up.

In 1801, Thomas Young gave us the famous double-slit experiment. The experiment involves sending a beam of light through two slits and onto a screen. What happens is the light goes through each slit and, as is expected of a light *wave*, it creates an interference pattern on a screen. A point for Huygens!

Not so fast. A problem occurs if you turn the light intensity down so far that you fire only a single photon of light through a single slit. What you get then is the behaviour of a *particle*. Newton gets the equaliser!

The real weirdness comes when you try and work out which slit the photon is going through, by adding an observer. Here, the light will switch between wave-like (interference) to particle-like (piles of particles) behaviour. Of course, neither Huygens nor Newton was the kind of person to find this celebration-worthy. It is, in fact, an unfortunate contradiction to all known laws of physics. How can something be both a wave *and* a particle? How can something completely change its being when it's observed a different way? The quantum world just flips and changes. It defies expectation with no obvious reason.

If I were a god with a sense of humour, that's exactly how I'd design the world.

Electromagnetism
All the Light You Can See

Electricity and magnetism, to the unscientific mind, are little different to magic. They are mysterious forces that, for most of human history, we could only gape at in wonder. But while we didn't know much about them, humans have long suspected the two are related. If you find yourself bored, you can do an experiment to prove it. Just place a magnet somewhere outside and wait until it gets struck by lightning. What you'll notice is that the magnet's polarity has been reversed. Which, to a pre-modern human, would have seemed pretty darn creepy.

It wasn't until the Danish scientist Hans Christian Ørsted came along at the beginning of the nineteenth century that we could prove more consistently that these two phenomena were connected. The (perhaps apocryphal) story goes that Ørsted was setting up an electric circuit to show some students its operation when he noticed a compass he had left nearby start to wobble. What he later discovered is that there's a magnetic field wrapped around every electric current. This was monumental. Shocked gasps and dropped conical flasks could be heard all around the world. Newton (and therefore all established physics) had failed to see this coming.

Some physicists have spent their lives trying to explain this, but the Englishman Michael Faraday just accepted it and moved on. What he discovered was that if you physically moved either a magnet or a conducting wire around each other, you can, essentially, produce an unlimited supply of electricity (provided things keep moving). It turns mechanical energy into electric energy. In the 1830s, Faraday created the first dynamo or electric generator – the basis of modern generators today.

Faraday also noticed that electromagnetism affected light, and hypothesised that light *was* electromagnetism, but couldn't support it. Enter James Clerk Maxwell (1831–1879). Maxwell discovered that the speed of propagation (movement) of electromagnetism is identical to the speed of light. Newton had thought of light as being made up of particles, and now Maxwell had offered a different perspective – everything we see and enjoy in the world is because of electromagnetism. (Although, today, we know that most things in physics can be seen as *both* particles and/or waves – see page 69.)

Seeing works a bit like this. Electromagnetic waves are bouncing around the world all the time. Occasionally, one will bounce to your eye. Since electrical fields are always wiggling and bouncing their 'charges' around, when they hit your retina, they disturb the charges inside. This, in turn, starts an electrical signal all along your optic nerve to your brain. Your brain is evolutionarily tuned to pick up a very narrow range of these signals, and so we 'see light' this way. Hypothetically, if we rewired the brain, our retinas are capable of giving us a whole new world of visual experiences.

So, the next time you enjoy a beautiful landscape, smile at your dog's wagging tail or gaze at your child's sleeping face, remember to thank electromagnetism.

The Earth
How Our Home Is Made

Spades out, everyone! We're going to do some digging. A lot of digging. I'll be honest, though, it's not going to be all fun. Eventually, after a few metres, the soil will turn to rock, so we're going to get a sweat on. But we've only 35km of the Earth's crust to get through. What's that between friends? After that, you'll need to don your heat suits because it'll be pretty spicy down there. The nearly 3000km mantle, composed of skin-meltingly hot, dense rock, might be a challenge. But don't worry, because after that we get a break from digging and get to swim! In the curative waters of bubbling iron and nickel. Take a deep breath, though, because we've got about 2000km to swim through. Then, phew! It's time to take a seat on the core of the planet – a thick ball of solid metal roughly the same size as the moon. Well done, team!

From the surface of the Earth, it's around 6400km to the centre. To put this into perspective, the deepest that humans have ever managed to go (with a robot underwater) is 35km. The sheer pressures inside the Earth are mind-boggling. Most of what we know about our planet's composition is proven by seismography: we can measure shock waves through liquid and solid sections of rock. But we can also infer from calculations what the Earth's composition *must* be like for it to behave as it does.

One such behaviour is all to do with magnetism. The Earth's inner core is molten liquid, and the swaying motion of this liquid acts as a kind of dynamo to create our electromagnetic fields – the north and south poles which twitch the needle of a compass. Mars, about 10 per cent of Earth's mass, is much cooler and doesn't have a liquid core. As such it has a very small magnetic field. Venus, on the other hand, is a similar size to Earth but rotates too slowly to create the dynamo effect necessary for electromagnetism. So we are fortunate to have our magnetic field. Without it, our ozone layers would be stripped away by cosmic winds. And without our atmosphere, the sun's radiation would have fried life before it had even got going.

How we understand our own planet is a huge step forward in our knowledge, not only giving us clues to the needs of life but also putting the universe into perspective. Hindu cosmology says the Earth is 155 trillion years old and Christianity says it's a young 6000. Science tells us it's about 4.5 billion years old. When we learn that our planet is a rock with a particular composition that gave rise to life-friendly conditions, then we can take stock of just how lucky we are. It's both unnerving to realise how fragile it all is but also quite nice to know that we, unique of all the planets (that we know of), are holding all the planetary trumps.

Thermodynamics and Entropy

The Relentless Decay of Time

Next time you go to a coffee shop, ask to have some milk in a separate jug. Take a seat, hunch over your brew and pour your milk in. Watch the patterns swirl. See the eddies, where white and black tumble together. Observe the second law of thermodynamics. In the dance of the milk you are witnessing entropy. You start with milk and a black coffee – neat and separate. When you put them together, you get chaos. The milk loses its milkiness and the black coffee loses its blackness – you get, instead, an entropic chimera known as the 'white Americano'.

The laws of thermodynamics are a cornerstone of classical physics. The first law of thermodynamics states that you can neither create nor destroy energy, you can merely move it around a bit (see Conservation of Matter, page 40). The second law, however, is something seemingly much more depressing. It tells us that everything will eventually break down. Energy will dissipate, hot things will cool and order will collapse into chaos. It's something we all know and witness all the time. When you open the front door and your mum says, 'You're letting the hot air out, you oaf!', that's entropy. When a birthday balloon eventually deflates to become a sad, wilted thing, that's entropy. When you drop an egg on the floor and cringe at the slimy, oozing mess, that's entropy.

We owe the word 'entropy' to the nineteenth-century German physicist Rudolf Clausius. The word comes from the ancient Greek words 'within' and 'transformation'. In any closed system (where there's no outside influence), what you see is a move from organisation to disorganisation. In our example, the coffee cup serves as the closed system.

The reason this is a big idea is that the second law of thermodynamics tells us that entropy will *always increase* (in a closed system and on average). Unless there's some jiggery-pokery involved, the milk particles in your coffee will not coalesce to reconstitute themselves. They're lost forever. If you put a hot-water bottle into your bed, the heat from the bottle will dissipate to warm the bed, and the bed will warm up from the bottle (until an equilibrium is reached). It doesn't *have* to be this way. Why not have a world where hot things just get hotter and cold things just get colder? Well, the law of thermodynamics.

Entropy is an irreversible one-way law. Things will always go from order to chaos. It's perhaps the best scientific account we can think of for 'time'. All the laws of physics are reversible in 'time' (in the same way a ball looks the same going up as coming down) with the exception of the second law of thermodynamics. Entropy means the arrow of time as we experience it. A life – both a human's and the universe's – is measured simply in how long it takes to break down.

Special Relativity
My Today, Your Tomorrow

You press a button and a light turns on. You shoot an arrow and it hits a target. You take some medicine and you feel better. Cause and effect. Then and now. Everything happens in a neat sequence so that we can move incrementally through time with an orderly 'past, present and future'. Time marches relentlessly on.

... That is, until Albert Einstein came along. Thanks to his theory of special relativity (published in 1905), scientists have challenged this 'Newtonian', fixed view of time. Instead, time is now seen as something that depends entirely on us, where we are and how fast we're moving.

Time is relative. You've probably heard that at some point, but what does it mean? Well, firstly, we have to know that the way we experience motion depends upon our specific perspective, or 'frame of reference'. For instance, as you're driving, it looks like cars on the other side are coming towards you. To those cars, you're coming towards them. To a person standing on the pavement, both cars are heading for each other. None of these perspectives is 'more right' than the others.

Now, since the speed of light is the same for us all, no matter where we are, *when* we experience an event will depend only on how long it takes the light to get to us. If you're moving away from an event, it will reach you later than it will reach me if I'm nearer to it (or if I'm moving away more slowly).

An event might seem to happen earlier for me because I'm nearer to it, and so it would then be my 'past' before it became your 'present'.

Another, slightly poignant, example is that some of the stars we see today could have died millions of years ago. To distant aliens living nearer them, those stars are ancient history. When we stare at the night sky, we're actually looking back in time.

To all intents and purposes, special relativity doesn't affect us too much. These effects are only apparent when things are moving close to the speed of light. But we're all human, going about our human business at human speed and on the same spinning rock. To us, a clock ticks, the sun rises and our hair still turns grey. Yet Einstein really did change the scientific world. Time had been seen as constant and true, and he showed it was neither. Relativity is what allows GPS (see page 228) and atomic clocks to be so precise. It's what lies at the heart of our understanding of nuclear energy production. Alongside this, relativity has also led to some fun questions for science fiction. For instance, if we were to see a spaceship travelling close to the speed of light, it would seem to us that they were moving and ageing incredibly slowly. I'm sure there's a Hollywood movie in there somewhere ...

Quantum Mechanics
Zombie Cats and Superheroes

Magic is a bit old hat, isn't it? We've had millennia of stories about enchanted stones and wandering wizards. Move over, hocus-pocus, now it's the era of *technobabble*. Today it's all about quantum-nano-singularity-multiversal-disparities.

'Gee, how did you become so strong?' says the boy to the superhero.

'Well, son, when the geospatial threads hyperscaled to entangle the quantum realities, I found my energy analytics to be supercharged.'

For a lot of people reading this, 'quantum' might as well mean 'magic'. It's the place where random stuff happens. It's a subatomic universe of photons 'wanting' to do things and waves deciding to behave like particles (see page 71), and everyone pretends that makes sense.

According to the Copenhagen interpretation (yes, even quantum physicists can't agree about quantum physics), there are three principles to the quantum world:

First, quantum objects – such as electrons, atoms or molecules – will change depending on if and how they are observed. This is the classic Schrödinger's cat metaphor, first devised in 1935. Imagine that we put a cat and some poison gas in a sealed box. Left closed and unobserved like this – as quantum objects are for the most part – the cat is *simultaneously* dead *and/or* alive. If you open the box and *observe* the cat, then this makes it *either* dead or alive. All quantum events are like this in that they become one thing only when observed in that way. (It's an often-missed point that Erwin Schrödinger deliberately made his analogy absurd to highlight how insufficient 'common sense' is when talking about the quantum world.)

The second principle is that nothing in nature is fixed ... it's a probability. The tiny quantum objects that make up your hand do not have a discrete, definable location but just areas they are more or less likely to be in – they can (and do) pop in and out of existence at random. Of course, the reason your hand doesn't disappear is that the statistical chance of all the billions and billions of particles in your hand disappearing *at the same time* is infinitesimally small.

The final principle is that we can never know all the values of a system *at the same time*. This is Werner Heisenberg's 'uncertainty principle' in action. For instance, you cannot observe both the momentum and location of a quantum object at the same time. The more precisely you measure one, the greater the uncertainty with which you can measure the other (and knowing both precisely is impossible).

Nothing I read about quantum physics makes me think it less than magical. If anything, it seems to be the *science* of magic. It's the scientifically acceptable position that something could levitate, disappear or turn into a frog (even if those are, statistically, quite unlikely). So, keep on trying to use the Force to attract the remote control. Quantum particles might make your day.

Bonding

Making Me Whole Again

If your partner or boss ever accuses you of being lazy, tell them that it's in your make-up. Because everything in the universe is lazy. All of the atoms that make up the world, from the light of distant stars to the skin under your fingernail, are lazy. They are trying to reach the lowest-energy state possible.

It's this simple fact about the universe that explains why chemicals come together or 'bond' to form complex structures. It was a twentieth-century breakthrough that would open a world of new technologies and allow us to understand how many materials behave – like why diamonds are so hard and which metals make for the best conductors.

Electromagnetism (see page 70) tells us that the entire world is governed by two charges: positive and negative. Inside every atom's nucleus there are a number of protons, which have a positive charge. These protons emit a kind of atomic call of the wild, shouting, 'Come to me, electrons of the world!' And this is because electrons are negatively charged. They hear this electromagnetic call and can't help but wiggle their way over. The reason they don't hop right into the nucleus gets pretty complicated – it depends on models, quantum-mechanical probabilities and angular momentum. Don't get it? Me neither.

Instead, thanks to kinetic energy, the electrons orbit the nucleus in shells or rings. In order for an atom to be the most 'stable' (i.e. in the lowest-energy state), all atoms 'want' to have a full outer shell of eight electrons (the inner shell has space for just two electrons, but only hydrogen and helium have the one shell). So, chemicals which have more or less than their full capacity of electrons in their outer shell are desperate to either offload their extras or get a few more. It's like a game of Happy Families, where you have to collect all the sets by swapping cards.

This happy collecting of electrons is called bonding. Hydrogen, for example, only has one electron in its outer shell, and oxygen has six. So, when you put two hydrogen atoms with an oxygen atom you get refreshing, low-energy and stable H_2O, also known as water. This is known as covalent bonding. There are other types of bonds (such as ionic, hydrogen, and London dispersion) but they all follow a similar principle.

Bonding is hugely important. Consider the oxygen we breathe: stable O_2. If you somehow managed to inhale a single oxygen atom, it would rip off bits from your tissue to try and find its absent electrons. Which sounds like a great science-fiction murder plot. The reason that chemical bonding is so important is that it allows variety and diversity in things (as 99 per cent of our solar system is made up from the bonding of just six elements). Everything you see and touch around you is a stable compound. It's lazy and content in its complete-outer-shell paradise.

Nuclear Energy
Unimaginable Potential

When most people think of the word 'nuclear', they think mushroom clouds, Chernobyl and Radioactive Man. 'Nuclear' is not a great brand – few people would buy nuclear toothpaste, nuclear biscuits or nuclear condoms. Technically, the word 'nuclear' is all about the 'nucleus' of an atom, but in practice, it's about energy. When scientists first learned how to split the atom in 1932, it opened up a world of potential – both for huge energy provision but also for the apocalypse (see page 296).

There are four 'fundamental forces' to the universe, the things that make everything work and do a lot of the heavy lifting in physics calculations. These forces are gravity (see page 67), electromagnetism (page 70), strong nuclear force and weak nuclear force. So, half of the fundamental building blocks of the universe deal with nuclear forces.

Nuclear *fusion* is probably the most important reaction in the entire universe – in fact, it was there at the start of the universe (see page 84). Without fusion, there would only ever be hydrogen. Fusion is what makes the sun the sun. And without the sun, there'd be no planets, no life and no lovely summer BBQs. Nuclear fusion happens when the nuclei of two lighter chemicals (like two hydrogen atoms) come together to form one heavier one – such as helium. Helium can, in turn, make carbon, which makes oxygen and so on. Fusion is what gives us the periodic table (see page 46) in all its variety.

This all sounds much easier than it actually is. Nuclei really *don't* want to join together, and so you need huge temperatures and pressures to make them do it – like at the centre of a star, for example. The interesting, and energy-making, fact about fusion is that when the two lighter nuclei join, the final mass of the heavier nucleus does not weigh the same as the sum of the two parts. There's missing mass. And this is what causes the immense energy we can potentially siphon off and use in reactors. Or we can let it loose to destroy entire cities – it's what makes the hydrogen bomb.

Nuclear *fission* is similar but the other way around. This is where a heavier nucleus splits to form two lighter ones. It's much easier to do but produces far less energy as a result. When I say, 'far less', I still mean energy enough to power the bombs that levelled Nagasaki and Hiroshima. In fact, *fission* is what hydrogen bombs use to give energy to the *fusion* mechanism. Hydrogen bombs today are 500 times more powerful than the ones used in the Second World War.

Nuclear energy is both a great destroyer and a great hope of the future. On the one hand, it has potential to resolve all of our energy crises and create a (potentially) safe and unlimited supply. But, on the other hand, it could vaporise us all in a thermonuclear explosion long before that.

The Big Bang
Neither Big Nor a Bang

Come on in! And welcome ... to the 'Before Time'! Take a deep breath, because there's not much oxygen in here. There's not much of anything, in fact. We're both incorporeally and incomprehensibly wobbling about in an absolute void. I'd say we've only been here for a short while, but time doesn't exist. I'd say it's quiet, but there's no noise. I think I'll just leave you to think up your own inadequate descriptors. Then, suddenly (a metaphorical time unit, of course), there's a bang. The most cosmos-defining bang you'll ever hear (metaphorical sound, of course). Stand agog, and witness the greatest thing in the history of the universe: the universe!

The Big Bang is a big deal in the history of ideas. It's the moment when science told us where the universe came from, and when (13.7 billion years ago, give or take).

Fred Hoyle, the astrophysicist who first coined the term 'Big Bang' in 1949, once said: 'Words are like harpoons. Once they go in, they are very hard to pull out.' Such is the case with 'Big Bang'. In 1993, a panel of scientists ran a competition to rebrand it. The problem was that 'Big Bang' was, as Timothy Ferris put it, 'inappropriately bellicose'. There are three things wrong with the term.

First, it implies an explosion of existing matter into pre-existing space. Yet the Big Bang theory says *all* matter, energy, space and time were jammed into an unimaginably small, dense universe. Second, 'Bang' implies violence, but there were no supernova firework displays. In fact, 'cosmic expansion' is a better name: a large balloon being blown up is a better mental image. Third, 'Big Bang' trivialises the idea. Hoyle, in fact, used it as a derogatory term, as he was debating *against* the idea.

In 1927, the Belgian Catholic priest and cosmologist Georges Lemaître published a compelling case for an expanding universe. But his work was mainly theoretical, and it was largely ignored. Other physicists (including Einstein) were all unhappy with existing 'origin' models of the universe but it wasn't until Edwin Hubble and his telescopic observations came along in 1929 that we cracked it. Essentially, Hubble noticed that (almost) all the stars were racing away from the Earth – the farther a galaxy is from us, the more of its light shifts to longer, redder wavelengths.

Ever since, we've been collecting more data in favour of the Big Bang theory. For instance, George Gamow, a Russian, showed how the current levels of hydrogen and helium in the universe provide further evidence. What's more, when we ended up exploring space (see page 226), we found cosmic microwave background radiation to push another pin in the Big Bang theorem board.

The Big Bang theory is controversial, particularly for those of a creationist bent. But awe and wonder do not stop with knowing things. Mystery does not die as the universe was born. In fact, the more you learn about theoretical physics (see page 88), the more wonder there is to find.

String Theory
One Rule to Bind Them All

People like answers. We want to know how a trick works, what's causing that odd sound in the car or who'll be revealed as the murderer in a thriller. It's why philosophers and scientists have always wanted to know what's 'behind' the universe. What indivisible bedrock scaffolds the world? In ancient Greece, Thales said it was water and Democritus said it was atoms. In China, sages thought it was chi. In the Vedas, it was Brahman. Today, the search for the fundamental substance of the universe goes on, but now it's called 'string'.

String theory is well intentioned but it walks the ever-blurry line between 'scientific theory' and 'belief'. Its entire reason for being is to unify all the known and existing science we have. So, at the moment, we have quantum mechanics to explain how really small things work (see page 78) and we have general relativity (which is Einstein's special relativity – see page 76 – extended to include gravity) to explain how the really big things work. The problem, though, is that if you try to apply one set of rules to the other (like quantum rules to the macrocosmic world) everything breaks down into a nonsense. Of course, the universe is not divided into two but is made up of both small and big things at the same time. So, to paraphrase the Dark Lord Sauron, we need one theory to rule them all and, in the darkness, bind them.

The One Ring of our modern speculative physics is string theory. String theory is the best answer we have to accommodate all of our confusing, competing science, and the theory says everything in the universe is made up of strings. Imagine you had a God-powered microscope and could look in on an electron. String theory says that what you would see is either an open or a closed string, oscillating to its own unique frequency across a great many dimensions. Those unique oscillations define what kind of particle it will be and what properties it will have.

The big issue with this is that there's not one quark's worth of evidence for string theory. It's debatable if it even counts as science because there's not (yet) been any meaningful way to test the theory (although some hope that the mysterious new science of 'black hole physics' might hold the answers). However, string theory does *much* more than simply make two rival ideas cohere. It offers a huge and new way of understanding the universe. It creates a great blanket re-understanding, in which quantum mechanics and general relativity play only a bit part.

Plus it's a cool theory, and it's the best one the scientific community has going for it. But, given how unproven it is, you might wonder if we're not better off just sticking with the ancient Indian Vedas.

Dark Matter and Energy
The Magic in the Universe

Physics, in its most extreme and theoretical hinterlands, looks a lot like philosophy. Because the moment you pause to think about dark matter and dark energy, it's hard not to feel a little spiritual. When physics lets loose, the mind wanders to quasi-religious, science-fiction conclusions.

The story of dark matter is one of mystery. It's thought that dark matter and energy together make up about 95 per cent of the universe, and we have no idea what they are.

Thanks to scientific developments like the Hubble telescope (launched in 1990), we can see galaxies far, far away. They also allow us to work out the mass of those galaxies. Which leaves physicists with a bit of a problem. Because, on the basis of these calculations, galaxies shouldn't look the way they do. If all there was to galaxies was observable matter, then what we know about gravity means that galaxies spinning around their centre should be spinning much more slowly towards their outskirts than they actually are. In short, we need about *five times* the amount of matter to explain the gravitational effects we can see.

It's a bit like placing a one-kilo bag of sugar into a cardboard box and closing the lid. Now, imagine you put this box onto some scales and find it weighs five kilos. You'd be a bit surprised. So, unable to peek inside the box, you would assume that at some point, somehow, some approximately four-kilogram *thing* got in there. We'd have to call it 'dark thing' to bring the analogy home.

That's dark matter. Dark *energy* we know about in a slightly different way. If we assume (as most physicists still do) that the universe began all at once (see page 84), then the rate at which things move away from us – observed via redshift – should be measured at specific speeds. But they're not: distant ones aren't the right kind of red and aren't going at the right kind of speed. This means the universe's expansion must be getting faster thanks to a *something* we don't know.

The analogy here might be if we were to imagine a tiny ant inflating a giant balloon. As pluckily determined as this ant might be, if it *succeeded* in blowing up the balloon, you'd probably assume it had some help. This help is dark energy.

When people learn about the concept of dark matter/energy, they tend to have one of two reactions. Either they're gobsmacked and awestruck. Suddenly the world has a magic to it that was thought extinguished by a cold, Enlightenment-stoked scientism. Or they're utterly unconvinced. An engineer I know once described it like this: 'Dark matter is what physicists invented because their calculations didn't add up.' Which is sure to irritate any physicists reading this book.

Whether you're a convert or an unbeliever, the fact is that dark matter poses huge and exciting new questions for our understanding of the universe. It makes me want to go back to university, to be honest.

The Simulation Hypothesis
Do You Think This Is a Game?

Every now and then, someone will say, 'But what if the world is just a simulation?!' And, even if we indulge the question a bit, we ultimately do the philosophical equivalent of rolling our eyes. 'Yes, mate,' we say, 'I practically grew up on *The Sims*, but let's not get carried away.' Yet might there be more to it than a late-night thought experiment?

This is what the contemporary philosopher Nick Bostrom claims in his 'simulation argument', and it's disturbingly convincing.

Our conscious mind is not actually that special. It's incredibly complex, and ridiculously powerful, but our brains ultimately just run a certain 'computational architecture'. We happen to have biological neurons, but really, the same system and structure would work perfectly well on silicon processors, too. So it's at least *possible* for a human mind to be run on a super-powerful computer (created, perhaps, by a sufficiently advanced civilisation).

So far, so generic. We've all seen *The Matrix*. However, what if we can show that a simulation is the *most likely* situation? Well, that would be something.

Bostrom's argument essentially boils down to this:

Even if the chances of developing super-powerful technology is tiny – say, one alien civilisation in every billion – and *even if* most civilisations, however advanced they get, wouldn't bother to simulate minds like ours, it's still overwhelmingly likely we're living in a simulation.

Why? Well, Bostrom uses probability theory. If we assume that there's a near-infinite number of possible civilisations in a near-infinite universe, it only takes one of them to be sufficiently advanced and willing to create simulated minds. And, given our most reasonable guess points to a universe really that large (if not actually infinite), the numbers add up – there's *bound* to be one.

So, we now know that it's overwhelmingly likely that at least one civilisation across all time has created a simulated universe. Once we've established that a civilisation *can* create simulated minds and a simulated universe as we know it (which, at the moment, seems impossible), then we have to assume there's practically no limit to how many they can create. It's like imagining how a computer game might spawn billions of 'minds' in a nanosecond.

This means that the universe is made up of 'real minds' and 'simulated by technology minds', and that there's far more of the latter. This being so, it's much more likely that *we're* one of the simulated minds than one of the biological super-advanced civilisations in the 'real' world.

So, thanks to the wonders of maths, we're overwhelmingly likely to be a simulation. How does that make you feel? Or will you wait for your feelings to be downloaded before you tell me?

Medicine

Most medicine, until modernity, was simply the sensible application of observable correlations. Eating this plant makes your stomach feel better, rubbing on this cream makes the rash go away and lancing that boil makes the swelling go down. Medicine was not about understanding how a drug worked – no one knew the causal agents involved, really – instead it was about trial and error. And you hoped you weren't the error. Today, of course, we know how (most) medicine works, and the future is hugely brighter for it.

Medicine is about curing the sick and keeping Death waiting a bit longer.

Traditional
Chinese Medicine
Very Ancient, Very Dubious

Up until the mid-sixteenth-century scientific revolution, each culture seemed to have its own medical approach. Without microscopes, there was no cellular pathology. Without cellular pathology, you were basically guessing based on correlations. For instance, we can all see that people get more colds in the winter, and colds produce phlegm. So, it's quite logical to believe that winter causes phlegm which causes the cold (hence humoral theory, see page 96). Physicians and herbalists would prescribe medications that worked most of the time, without knowing why – cloves for toothache, willow bark for arthritis or chalk for indigestion. By trial and error, bumbling and groping, folk medicine kind of did okay.

Traditional Chinese medicine (TCM) has always been one of the most widespread forms of cultural medicine (not least because China is huge). It's a practice that still dominates for much of the world's population today.

It's often assumed that 'ancient' correlates to 'wise' – like an old codger on a bench who's seen it all and can give us some nuggets of wisdom. And, in folk

Chinese medical practices, there's some of that. Acupuncture, for instance, has been proven to work in certain cases – like for those with back pain or arthritis. Likewise, tai chi (detached from its Daoist spiritual components, see page 286) can work wonders for general fitness, mental health and pain relief. Various herbs and concoctions passed down through the millennia contain active ingredients that we now know help with some ailments.

So, there is *some* profound knowledge to be found in the ways of our forebears. For most of the time, though, old ways are best kept old. Many 'traditional herbal remedies' are, at best, little more than placebos. At worst, they can have upsettingly lethal side effects.

Today, TCM is formalised by the Communist Party of China, which releases, annually, its *Chinese Pharmacopoeia*. This is a recipe book for all the drugs and formulae your traditional home pharmacist needs. Like some Heston Blumenthal nightmare, it teaches you how to make medicines using dried placenta, flying squirrel poo and, of course, lots of snake oil.

The problem is that the *Pharmacopoeia* also contains recipes that require ingredients from rare or endangered animals. Leopard bones for health tonics, pangolin scales for blood conditions and, recently, bear bile for COVID-19 (extracted with difficulty and distress for the bear) – are all in high, and expensive, demand. With an estimated *2.5 billion* people following TCM, that's a big, extinction-level problem.

In many ways, TCM is the story of many of the technologies or ideas described in this book. When it's used properly or well, there's little harm in it, and possibly even benefit to be had. But when harnessed for profit with no care for its effects, it is very bad indeed.

Humoral Theory
Bloody Phlegm and Bilious Pus

The science of a previous age can seem absurd to us today. When a paradigm shifts, it's hard to imagine how people formerly believed such nonsense. Yet if we were to explain to a time-travelling Roman our current microbial theory, which maintains that invisible germs are battling with white blood cells floating around our body, they'd think we were a few denarii short of a treasure chest.

So what *did* they believe?

Humoral theory was first developed by the ancient Greeks, notably Hippocrates, but was popularised (and spread over the Roman Empire) by the Roman physician, Galen. It came to dominate Western medieval medicine for more than a millennium, and echoes of it can still be found in our language and even in how we think.

Galen believed the body was divided into four separate 'humours'. These were phlegm, blood, black bile and yellow bile. Good health, then, came in balancing these humours in the body. Have you got the flu? Then get rid of phlegm! Feeling headachy? Leech some blood! Feeling melancholic? Drink this tonic of bile! Suffering from blood loss? Leech some more blood! (This last isn't even made up.)

It's not hard to understand how the theory emerged. As we see all too frequently, humans, even today, often confuse symptoms with causes.

The humours, though, were more than simply biological fluids, and they came to be associated with seasons, elements, organs, character traits and even astrology. An entire folklore developed out of them. Spring would produce 'good blood', and so we'd become happy and healthy. Winter, the cold and flu season, quickly became associated with phlegm. Black bile was associated with the spleen and blood with the heart. Yellow bile was associated with fire, and phlegm with water. Blood was aligned with Jupiter, phlegm with the moon. And so on. Humoral theory permeated an incredible depth of everyday thought.

Today, English still contains words that relate to humoral theory. We can call someone 'phlegmatic' (level-headed), 'sanguine' (cheerful and optimistic – from the Latin for blood), 'bilious' (bad-tempered) and 'melancholic' (depressive – from the Greek for 'black bile').

Humoral theory was still the accepted norm as late as the nineteenth century but was eventually displaced by the advent of cellular pathology. Today, the idea sounds more like certain Eastern concepts such as *chi*. It also echoes across various homoeopathic and New Age beliefs. However, as you can imagine, leeching for nigh-on every disease was unlikely to succeed on its own.

Voltaire once said (one of my favourite quotations): 'The art of medicine consists of amusing the patient while nature cures the disease.' The long-lasting success of humoral theory stands testament to that idea.

97

Anaesthesia
Pain-free and (Usually) Not Dead!

You wake up from a fitful, agitated sleep. Your foot is getting worse and it's started to ooze a horrid yellow goo. The year is 1710 and gangrene is not fun. The doctor gave you two options: live with the pain and eventually die or have the foot amputated. Today, with our general anaesthetics and post-operative codeine, the choice seems a pretty obvious one. Sure, you'll miss your foot but it's better than dying. But in 1710, an operation meant getting paralytically drunk, being tied down and hoping you passed out from the pain. If you got through that, then your pain relief consisted of more booze, Mrs Taylor's magic herbs or an Arabic potion that might help but might make you go blind.

I think most of us will agree that we're better off with modern anaesthesia.

If you want to knock someone out, you pretty much have four methods at your disposal (all of which were used by surgeons in history). One, you strangle them, cutting off their oxygen just enough for them to pass out but not pass away. Two, you freeze them, since lowering your body temperature enough brings on a hypothermic coma. Three, you get someone big to punch them in the head. (Publisher's note: do not try any of these methods at home.) Four, the most boringly modern option, you use chemicals.

For most of the Middle Ages, people stewed all sorts of potions as anaesthetics. Mandrake, nightshade, opium, saw-wort, henbane and cannabis are all naturally found anaesthetics. These were either consumed or soaked on a 'soporific sponge' and wafted around your face. If this was done well, your operation was a pain-free miracle. If done badly, it worked not at all. If done *very* badly, there would be no need for the operation ...

All this changed with ether. In the sixteenth century, it was discovered that you can make ether from ethanol and sulphuric acid, and physicians were quick to note its pain-relieving qualities. But it was only when it was reformulated into a vapour that it made people really forget their pain. Likewise, laughing gas – nitrous oxide – not only made people giddy and slightly high but also numbed them enough to make dentistry and surgery a tiny bit less torturous (if not, itself, a laughing matter).

Ether and nitrous oxide did passably well for a while, but what people really wanted was a 'knockout' formula. Chloroform did the job but given the eye-bulging mortality rates, it wasn't long before safer, and more effective, gases were utilised. Today, the medical profession tends to use a mixture of nitrous oxide and either sevoflurane, halothane, isoflurane or desflurane, while propofol is used for intravenous anaesthesia. There'll be a test on those at the end.

Anaesthesia is still not an easy or risk-free business, but with only roughly one in 200,000 dying from operations these days, it's much safer than Mrs Taylor's magic herbs.

Vaccinations

Saving Lives Since 1796

Humans are mucky, yucky and grubby. So, when you jam us together in dense cities with dubious sanitation facilities, you often get a lot of disease. Since the earliest civilisations came together to form big cities (see page 133), humans have lived with near-constant cycles of plagues.

And so when Edward Jenner (1749–1823) developed the first vaccine, the world breathed a sigh of relief. In our modern world, where a tiny fraction of people have to worry about diseases for most of their life, we forget just how valuable vaccinations are.

Smallpox was, once, one of the most terrible and fatal of diseases. The European strain, known as variola minor, would regularly kill 1–3 per cent of the population. But in Asia, it was much worse, with a mortality rate as high as 50 per cent. It was shockingly common.

Before Jenner, people in various parts of the world were dealing with smallpox by 'inoculation'. This is when someone is given a live dose of the virus which is hopefully mild or weak enough to cause only a slight sickness, after which they'll then be immune.

Needless to say, this was risky business, not least because there was no way to guarantee the infection would be slight. This is why Edward Jenner was so important.

Jenner was an English country doctor who tended mostly to farming communities. During his work he noticed how dairymaids – those who milked cows – rarely, if ever, got smallpox. But he observed that these women *did* have blisters or scars on their hands from cowpox. Without knowing the science at all, Jenner hypothesised that this cowpox strain must be a weaker version of smallpox, which in some way immunised the dairymaids from the more serious illness.

In a follow-up experiment that would land him in jail today, Jenner infected his gardener's son with cowpox, then, after a while, the smallpox virus. It was a huge success – for Jenner, for the young boy (fortunately) and for humanity.

Early vaccinations were dirty and definitely not risk-free, yet people *still* took them up. People weighed up the much worse risk of smallpox against the risk of a badly done vaccination and saw vaccinations for the good they were.

In the decades and centuries that followed Jenner, scientists learned to first weaken the inoculating virus (like in the MMR vaccine), and in some cases (like polio vaccines) kill the virus altogether. Vaccinations today are overwhelmingly safe, quick and easy. They protect us from crippling, scarring and fatal illnesses. The growth of anti-vaccination conspiracy theorists today is ironically a symptom of vaccine success – we've been free from serious epidemics for so long that we hardly remember how much we needed this remarkable medical breakthrough.

Antiseptics

Mr Lister

Inside my bathroom cabinet lies an homage to one of the greatest scientists in medical history. 'Listerine', the cheek-burning, breath-freshening mouthwash, is so named after Joseph Lister (1827–1912) – the father of antiseptics. When Listerine was launched with the slogan 'Kills the germs that cause bad breath', it was a nod to the original carbolic acid Lister used to sterilise medical instruments. And now, every time I swish and swirl my mouthwash, I give ritual thanks to Mr Lister.

Because without him, I'd likely be dead.

Every moment of every day you are being bombarded by pestilential opportunists. There are more than 3,000 bacteria on your hand, right now. A door handle will have fourteen different colonies of bacteria, and your computer mouse is five times dirtier than your toilet seat. The world is full of bugs and viruses that are desperate to get inside your warm, wet, sugar-rich bloodstream. Thank heavens, then, for your skin. The outer barrier of your skin is a densely packed layer of dead cells. Disgusting, yes, but also protective. Your skin's natural oil, called sebum, is antimicrobial and inhibits bacterial growth, and when you sweat, thousands of germs are washed away. And if you graze yourself, your body will seal off the area (with a scab) while your skin gets to work repairing itself. Thanks, skin!

But, sometimes, like if you need an operation of any kind, a surgeon will need to pierce your skin. This might be good in the short term, but that incision is like the *Starship Enterprise* letting down its forcefields.

For much of history, when a surgeon cut you open, they risked your life in two ways. First, they opened your body to airborne invaders. Second (and probably more lethally), their surgical tools pushed bacteria and viruses deep inside your tissue. They did the pathogens' work for them. Some of this was anecdotally known. Florence Nightingale recognised a correlation between cleanliness and health: by filling wards with fresh air and clean equipment, she reduced the risk of germs getting inside all those Crimean war wounds. Likewise, the Hungarian obstetrician Ignaz Semmelweis advocated handwashing, and the British chemist William Henry tried to sterilise clothes with heat.

But it was Joseph Lister who revolutionised antiseptics. Lister knew his germ theory (see page 26) and invented a carbolic-acid sprayer that killed nearly all microbes on a surface. Lister's use of antiseptics was simple, good science. He disinfected his medical equipment and studied the outcomes, publishing his research in 1867. Thanks to Lister, deaths from post-operative infection went from 60 to 4 per cent. That's thousands of lives saved every year.

Today, no (reputable) operation is performed without antiseptics. On the back of a global pandemic, we all keep a few antiseptic hand gels nearby. We're germ-conscious and often germ-afraid. And we're much less likely to die because of that.

Caesareans
Cutting Mortality

I bet you know someone who has had a caesarean section. It's thought around 20 per cent of childbirths in the world today involve birth by operation. C-sections have been common for centuries, but the noticeable difference, today, is that the mothers are still alive when they have them. Up until the invention of modern antiseptics (see page 102), a caesarean was almost certainly a death sentence. And so they were only ever performed on women already dead. If you see a medieval epithet 'the fortunate', 'the unborn' or 'not born of a woman' – it means they were a caesarean baby. Likewise, the names Nonnatus or Ingenito.

The fact that so many successful caesarean sections happen today is not only a medical marvel, it's also a reminder of how dangerous childbirth was for pretty much all of human history.

Up until the 1600s, a pregnant mother had between a 1–2 per cent chance of dying in childbirth. Given that most people in those days would have upwards of five children, that meant a mother could have a 10 per cent chance of dying young. The sad reality is that for many people in the developing world these numbers are still true. But, as bad as mother mortality was (is), the risk of an unborn infant dying during childbirth was (is) even higher.

The caesarean section is just one way we've turned those statistics around. Historically, the C-section has been linked to salvation. The medieval Christian Church insisted on a caesarean if there was a chance the unborn baby could be saved after a mother's death – for baptismal purposes. Because of the urgency of the situation, it's one of the few operations where midwifes were permitted to perform major surgery. What's more, because the newborn would, tragically, have a low chance of survival, the midwives were also given baptismal powers. A rare instance of early female empowerment.

The modern C-section (which began in the 1940s) thankfully has far better outcomes, but it's still major surgery. C-sections are often used when either the mother's or child's life is at risk due to a medical complication. The operation, done properly, is often safer than vaginal births in these circumstances.

But they are not without controversy. In some developed counties like the USA, hospitals are accused of overusing C-sections (doctors get paid much more for them by medical insurers), sometimes against the mother's wishes. The World Health Organisation recommends between 10–15 per cent of births ought to be by caesarean section, given probabilities of complications. In the US, it's 31 per cent. In Brazil, it's 40 per cent.

Maternal choice is important, but, in the grand sweep of history, the existence of the C-section is far, far more beneficial than not. It's saved countless mothers and children, and many people reading this would not be alive if it weren't for their use.

X-rays
Halloween Hands

One thing that unites all the great philosophers, scientists and inventors of history is curiosity. If something mysterious happened to me, I'd probably shrug and say, 'Oh, that was weird', and go about my life. The genius, though, never accepts an unturned stone or unopened door. It's this insistent curiosity that we have to thank for the invention of one of the most revolutionary inventions in medicine: the X-ray.

In 1895, the German physicist Wilhelm Conrad Röntgen was experimenting on lightbulbs. Boring work, really, but important nonetheless. As Röntgen was working with a cathode ray tube, he noticed a strange and previously unseen type of radiation emitting from the tube. What was even more peculiar was that, as he was later experimenting on this new ray, he saw, on a screen, the ghostly flicker of the bones in his hand. Later that year, a few days before Christmas, Röntgen tried the trick on his wife, causing her to shout, 'I have seen my own death!' Quite the festive hoot at the Röntgen house.

Since these rays were unknown, Röntgen called them 'X' rays (in some circles they were actually called 'Röntgen rays' for a while), and over a century later we live every day with his miraculous, mysterious discovery. X-rays were first used in medicine and dentistry just two weeks after Röntgen published his findings, but of course, no one knew then what damage they did. It's a genuine surprise it took years before people realised the increasing incidences of skin burning and bleeding might be caused by the heavier dosages of X-rays being used in hospitals. In 1908, one of the first surgeons to take up X-rays, John Hall-Edward, had to have his arm amputated because of the damage.

X-rays are essentially electromagnetic radiation composed of photons. Photons can penetrate the soft tissues of our bodies but not the harder bits inside (like bones or teeth or random objects in random orifices). Today, we've managed to make X-rays as safe as possible, so long as you don't take too many in too short a time.

In ancient Greece, the word *pharmakon* meant both poison and remedy. It was thought most curatives would become toxic if taken in the wrong proportions. This is certainly the case with X-rays. At low levels, they are an invaluable diagnostic tool, but in large doses, they become carcinogenic monsters. But the twist in this tale is that the ingenuity of humans has harnessed the poison. Because while X-rays can destroy skin and organs, they can also destroy *tumours*. Today, we use radiation therapy (see page 109) to cure certain cancers.

The best thing about the story of X-rays is that it's one of the 'Oh, wow' moments of accidental discovery. It keeps alive the idea that some amateur scientist or lab technician might, tomorrow, stumble across an absolutely game-changing invention.

Cancer Treatments

Just Another Disease

If you had to do a task over and over again, for years and years, I'd bet you'd drop the ball here and there. So, too, with the cells in your body. All of them are locked in a cycle of growth, division and death. Since you started reading this page, around 150 million cells in your body have died. If you're over fifty, a proportion of those will not be replaced. Since you were born, your cells have replicated themselves an unfathomable number of times. It's a wonder, then, that there isn't *more* cancer. Cancer is when the cells slip up – they divide uncontrollably and forget to switch off. They grow, and grow, and consume everything around them. Eventually, these masses form tumours. Eventually, these tumours will kill you.

But cancer is not the number-one enemy it once was and is no longer the taboo of yesteryear. In fact, it's so common that around half of us are likely to get it. *All* of us will get it if we live long enough.

Before the modern period, cancer was not well documented. Most people died before the age when cancer develops, and tumours were often thought to be caused by other conditions. From the eighteenth century onwards, we find more accounts of cancer, but its treatment involved clutching at straws.

In 1713, the Italian doctor Bernardino Ramazzini noted that nuns had a high prevalence of breast cancer. He speculated it was down to a lack of sex and, in a roundabout way, he was right. Today, we know that women who have children are less likely to develop breast cancer – but we still don't know why.

The only chance of combating cancer before the modern period was surgery to remove tumours. Before the mid-nineteenth century, this meant no antiseptic and you would very likely have died from the operation. When surgery underwent its hygienic revolution in the 1800s, things got a bit better – but success depended (as today) on how early the cancer was detected and what type it was.

Within a few months of the first X-rays (see page 106), doctors noticed that the radiation shrank or killed certain skin tumours. And so X-rays were quickly adapted to be cancer-killers. In the early days, patients were overwhelmed with a barrage of radiation, which caused them to burn and bleed. Radiotherapy, since the nineteenth century, has been all about tinkering with dosage and targeting.

The third big advance in cancer treatment was chemotherapy in the 1910s. Chemotherapeutic drugs are designed to kill cells – both cancerous and healthy. As with radiotherapy, the early versions were slapdash and deadly. Over time, they have become better balanced and their application refined.

Today, cancer is most often just a disease and not a death sentence. Almost everyone reading this book will know someone who's had cancer. Most will know someone who's come through it. And, historically, that makes this a very lucky time in which to live.

Modern Medicine
The Case for 'Big Pharma'

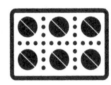

Most households have a 'pharmacy cabinet'. It's that shelf, probably in your bathroom, overflowing with half-opened ibuprofen, paracetamol and antihistamines. You probably don't appreciate just how abnormal this is in the history of humanity. If you were thrown back even a few centuries in time, you'd have to rely on the 'apothecary' for all your headache-relieving needs.

Of course, your local apothecary might not always be reliable. Their special 'nostrum' (a medicine made to a secret in-house recipe) might be little more than sugar water. Or it might dissolve your innards. Your choice to go either to the apothecary, a physician or your mate in the pub depended largely on your finances and your penchant for risk. Which is why pharmaceutical regulation, and then large-scale drug-production, is so important. Not only did it make medicine safer, but it brought it to the masses.

If the sixteenth and seventeenth centuries were a bubbling, lava pool of science, then the nineteenth century was the eruption. It was then that chemists learned how to synthesise chemicals, biologists discovered various diseases (and their cures) and industrialists invented new ways to produce more things in less time (see page 146). From out of this came the big companies we still know today, like Merck in Germany, Pfizer in the US and Beecham in the UK.

One of the first drugs to be mass-produced was aspirin. Aspirin was first invented and patented by the German drug company Bayer, which was a nuisance for the rest of the pharmaceutical industry because it was medicinal gold dust. Lucky for them, then, that the First World War happened. Bayer's legal trademark ran out bang in the middle of the war, which allowed other companies, especially American ones, to deny them its renewal. 'We can't possibly allow a *German* company to have this kind of financial monopoly,' they said. And so they quickly, and profitably, stole the patent.

It soon became obvious that being the first to invent and then trademark a new drug was the best way to turn a few (million) bucks. It's a genuine story of capitalistic success – as shareholders got richer, the world got healthier. We got quinine (for malaria), aspirin and various vaccines in the nineteenth century, insulin, vitamin C and penicillin in the twentieth. Today, a company that discovers or invents a drug has around twenty years with the patent. Twenty years to dominate the market, get ahead of the game and turn the brand name (e.g., Viagra) into mainstream lexicon.

It's easy to attack the wealth, power and cynicism of the pharmaceutical industry. They have been known to peddle lies and fund dubious research, among other practices. But without 'big pharma' there'd be a lot more suffering in the world. Imagine even a single year without being able to use anything in your bathroom cabinet? No toothpaste, no pain relief and no contraceptive pill (see page 58). A different world indeed.

Psychiatry
Pulling Up What Lies Below

'A worse plague cannot happen to a man, than to be so troubled in his mind', wrote Robert Burton in his great – if wordy – *Anatomy of Melancholy* (1621). Burton's poignant account of his mental health resonates through the ages – because depression, like many mental illnesses, is at the core of human existence. Burton's book is just one of many examples that challenge the narrative that psychiatry is a purely twentieth-century invention. True, it was only after the likes of Alfred Adler and Sigmund Freud started practising that the idea of 'mental health' took off, but it's incorrect to say that older cultures had no knowledge of the concept.

That said, many early attempts to understand mental illness were surface-deep. It's often the case that when humans don't understand how something works, they explain it with magic. With no real understanding of the human brain, early medical practitioners suggested that the mentally ill must be possessed by demons, have a misbalance in their humours (see page 96) or have irritated the wrong god.

But some cultures dug a little deeper. The Indian Vedas talk of mental balance across three *gunas* (energies). The Chinese text *The Yellow Emperor's Classic of Internal Medicine* explicitly lists mental illness as akin to physical. Ancient Egyptians thought mental health resided in the heart – not quite modern psychiatry but definitely a biological approach to the issue. The first use of the term 'mentally ill' probably dates back to the early-sixteenth-century's Johann Weyer (who had little time for superstition). People like Galen, Ibn Sina, René Descartes, Thomas Willis and William Battie each advanced our understanding of mental health – all pre-modern, and all doing psychiatry of a sort.

But the psychiatric landscape as we understand it today is defined by the Austrians. Josef Breuer (1842–1925), one-time mentor to Freud, successfully treated an 'Anna O' with a version of a talking cure. He pulled up, examined and sought to rationalise Anna's problems. But only one man gets called 'the father of psychology': Freud. Freudianism starts with the fundamental belief that we have certain unconscious drives, most of which are in conflict. The tension between these drives is what makes people 'neurotic', and so various therapies, like guided reflections, are necessary to rebalance the mind. Unsurprisingly, his first major book, *The Interpretation of Dreams* (1899) – with its themes of infantile sexuality, repressed libido, unconscious drives and a divided self – was hugely controversial for a readership in suits and corsets.

There are still Freudian psychiatrists today, but Austrian-style psychotherapy has fallen out of favour and often plays second fiddle to the more empirically successful disciplines of cognitive behavioural therapy (CBT) and mindfulness. We are all more aware of mental health and understand the physiological and neuroscientific reasons behind it. Despite that, though, it's still probably best not to irritate the wrong god.

Antibiotics

Don't Eat Mouldy Bread

You've come to Alex's for tea. It's all been pretty pleasant so far – gentle chit-chat, comfy seats, and you love a nice biscuit. After a while, Alex stands up.

'Let me show you something,' he says. Five minutes later, he's back, with an item in his hand. You squint to see what he's got. *Oh, good grief. Not again, Alex.*

'Look at my bacteria plates!' he says, wafting his dirty crockery. But, interrupting his usual monologue, suddenly he frowns.

'Why the devil aren't bacteria growing here?' A long pause, then: 'By Jove! This tiny bit of mould is killing my bacteria!'

This is the story of one of the greatest life-saving discoveries in history.

Alexander Fleming was lucky. If you decided to eat mouldy bread or cheese as an antibiotic substitute, you'd probably get more ill, not less. There are many types of mould, and only one – penicillium – contains the extractable element that Fleming needed for penicillin (he originally called the extract 'mould juice', which I wish was the market name today). Penicillin works essentially by making certain bacteria cells (gram-positive bacteria) fragile and porous. Eventually, these bacteria explode, making them much easier for your immune system to mop up.

Penicillin was nature's game changer, but it was human ingenuity that changed the world ... though that human wasn't Alexander Fleming. Fleming used penicillin to cure one eye infection; he wrote his findings up in 1929 and then returned to his first love: vaccines.

Ten years later, at Oxford University, Howard Florey and Ernst Chain (a Jew who had fled from Nazi Germany) read Fleming's paper and were intrigued. It was Florey and Chain who did the proper research and wide experimentation. In 1941, the first human trial took place using a man with a terrible infected scratch on his face. The penicillin reversed the infection and the subject started getting better ... but then the supply ran out and the trial ended. The man succumbed again and died. (Today, these infections are vanishingly rare because of antibiotics.) But in all the full trials that came afterwards it was clear: penicillin did the job!

After this, the world was on the hunt for more productive penicillium strains. Oddly enough, the best – to this day – was found on a mouldy cantaloupe in an Illinois market. Improved laboratory production techniques (like using UV light on the mould) meant that penicillin was soon being used to combat a great many previously fatal diseases, from pneumonia to syphilis.

Penicillin and the antibiotics that came after it have eradicated former killers like smallpox and (nearly) tuberculosis. Antibiotics make possible long, dangerous operations – like organ transplants and heart surgery – without the risk of infected wounds. And it's all down to one of the greatest scientific accidents of all time. As the (modest) Fleming said, 'I did not invent penicillin. Nature did that. I only discovered it by accident.'

Psychedelics
Open the Doors of Perception

If I offered you something that would likely be one of your most meaningful experiences ever, would you take it? What if I could guarantee to give you an enhanced awareness, so that everything was more vivid and incredible? If you could have a mystical experience on a whim, would you do it?

Welcome to the world of psychedelics.

Aldous Huxley's *The Doors of Perception* (1954) is an account of his trip on the psychoactive drug mescaline. Huxley had long been fascinated by Eastern religions and transcendence of the self. He'd had slight success with meditation but decided to take a 'chemical surrogate' to induce an 'at oneness' with the world.

Over eight hours, Huxley first enjoys the new intensity and depth in his experience of everyday sensations. Then he falls into what most would call a mystical experience. He sees the universe in a bunch of flowers, and, in them, 'a transience that was yet eternal life, a perpetual perishing that was at the same time pure Being ... the divine source of all existence'.

We all seek to lose ourselves sometimes. In fact, it seems to be part of the human condition: almost all known societies have their own particular hallucinogens. Psychedelics are found across all ages, not least in our modern addictions to alcohol, tobacco and marijuana. Should we see that as a problem? If mystical experience or transcendence is, as Huxley says, 'a principal appetite of the soul', why would we deny people the transformative power of psychedelic drugs if religion no longer provides this experience for most people? The elevated awareness of a trip, according to Huxley, is of 'inestimable value to everyone', so why not make it widely available?

Of course, there are risks. Suicides and accidents might increase, and there's a 1 per cent chance of psychosis. But does this risk mean we ought to ban something that gives two-thirds of everyone else their most meaningful experiences ever, according to some studies? And which has been a constant throughout human history?

Tobacco gives us lung cancer and alcohol 'results in brawls, crimes of violence and traffic accidents', Huxley writes. Psychedelics give people meaningful, mystical and profound encounters that 'shake us from the ruts of ordinary perception'. If we could experience the 'divine order of things' or feel at one with the world, why would we *not* do that?

Transplants
Lend Me Your Ears and I'll Give You a Hand

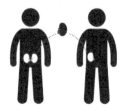

The more you learn about the human body, the more of a Frankenstein's monster it seems. Apart from the mysterious, over-achieving brain, our bodies really aren't that special. A few pints of blood, a nervous system (see page 18) and various lumps of tissue that we call 'organs'. When you get down to it, we're not too much different to an old, well-loved car. And, like a car, the more mileage you get under your belt, the more things start to creak. The heart weakens, the lungs get less efficient and your kidneys will shrink. And if death is, essentially, when your organs run out of steam, why not keep the reaper at bay with a new set?

The invention of transplants has been a life-extending, viscerally revitalising breakthrough.

That the skin is the largest organ in the body seems like one of those cheat facts, but it's also pedantically true. So, since we're doing a 'history of transplants', it would be an oversight not to mention skin grafts. Hindu sources from 3,000 years ago tell us of successful nose-skin transplants, with skin taken from the executed dead. The Roman Celsus (died c. 50 AD) even described a way to recreate a circumcised foreskin using existing peripheral skin (we're told the operation is much easier if you have a small penis).

The first (non-cheat) transplant was of the cornea – which is that dome-shaped thing in front of your pupil. In 1905, the Austrian Eduard Zirm took the corneas from a blind boy and sewed them onto Alois Glogar's broken eyes using conjunctiva tissue (isn't this a lovely entry?). The cornea is unique in having an 'immune privilege' because of a high concentration of immunosuppressive chemicals in its anatomy, which is why it made for a perfect 'first transplant'.

The first large, invasive 'organ transplant' was when a twin donated a kidney to his brother in 1954. Kidneys fail because of high blood pressure, diabetes or some genetic malformation. When transplanting a kidney, the original, weaker kidney is often left in place as well – so you can actually have up to five kidneys at once. The dysfunctional ones shrivel up to be very small.

But organ transplants were still a high-risk, last-resort operation until the invention of immunosuppressant drugs in the 1960s. Before this, most donated organs were rejected, the body viewing them as parasites – which is why a twin's kidney had more chance of success. After this, we had transplant milestone after milestone: lung (1963), pancreas (1966), liver (1967) and heart (1967).

For many people, the first heart transplant was an epochal moment. Throughout history, the heart was seen as delicate, the mystical seat of the soul. Its beat defined who we are. Then, faced with the possibility of living with another person's heart, we were forced to re-evaluate what being a human meant. All at once, the human body became considerably less magical, and much more mechanical, than it had been before.

IVF

Hope Where There Was None

We can all understand loss. Most of us have mourned the death of someone close to us, and have spent time in the wintry chrysalis of grief. We miss our loved ones, and we imagine we can hear their voice or feel their touch. Grief is the remembrance of an emptiness once filled. But how can we understand the loss of something we never had? How can we mourn what we never knew?

Most people want children. Having kids is such a fundamental part of our collective narrative (for better or worse), that when someone finds out they *can't* have children, it can be devastating. Historically, this has been made worse by the baggage associated with infertility. Infertility once meant shame. A childless woman meant a failed woman. 'Barren' was a loaded word. The result was depression, isolation and often much worse.

Of course, not *everyone* wants children, but for the millions who do, but can't (roughly 10–15 per cent of the population have fertility problems – it is far, far more common than you might think), IVF offers hope. IVF stands for *in vitro* fertilisation, and *in vitro* means 'in glass', which is why IVF children used to be called 'test-tube babies'. The first IVF pregnancy was a rabbit in 1959, and, in 1978, the world got its first IVF human in the form of Louise Brown.

Louise's birth was made possible by two British gynaecologists, Dr Patrick Steptoe and Dr Robert Edwards. Steptoe developed better ways to stimulate and retrieve eggs, and Edwards improved the method for fertilising those eggs *in vitro*.

IVF works in three stages. The first involves hormonal therapy to stimulate the mother's ovaries and develop multiple eggs. The second uses a needle and suction device to retrieve those eggs. The third step has the eggs fertilised and cultured for several days, before the most viable embryo is transferred to the woman's uterus to develop into a pregnancy (ideally after five days). In the 1970s, IVF had around a 10 per cent chance of success. Today, for women under thirty-five, it's nearer 40 per cent.

There are about eight million IVF babies alive today. That's roughly the population of Switzerland. But there are problems, too. First, it's very, very expensive, and so disqualifies any parents unable to pay or without insurance (or who don't qualify for the treatment under the NHS). Second, there are certain ethical issues – what becomes of discarded embryos? And what potential is there for science-fiction, dystopian, genetically modified babies? Third, success is still far from guaranteed – most IVF attempts still end in failure, with chances diminishing with age. But overwhelmingly, IVF has been an idea for the good. It's given joy and hope to people all over the world – for those struggling with fertility, and single or same-sex parents, too. It's given the world more love.

Nanotechnology
The Future's Here, the Future's Nano

Science fiction is full of tropes: lasers, teleporters, quantum entanglement, cyborgs and, of course, *nanotechnology*. When you learn about nanotech, it becomes obvious why this is. It's absolutely incredible. For something which, technically, began only seventy years ago, it definitely seems futuristic. As with a lot of brilliant, disruptive new tech, it is simultaneously dystopian and utopic. The idea of your body swarming with molecular-sized technology, fixing you up and mending you, sounds both great and disturbing.

'Nano' effectively means 'mind-bogglingly small'. It's anything that operates at a molecular level. The big advantage of using nanotechnology in medicine is that at this level things behave very differently to their composite counterparts – for instance, targeting a molecule that makes up a cancer is an entirely different ballgame to taking on the cancer itself.

There are, broadly, two kinds of medicinal nanotech – organic and inorganic. Organic nanoparticles are chemicals which are often used in drug delivery. A good example of this is the ongoing battle with antibiotic resistance. Antibiotics (see page 114) have undoubtedly saved millions of lives. But bacteria have billions of years of evolutionary practice at adapting to hostile immune systems, and they are fighting back. In the USA, around 3 million people a year are infected with antibiotic-immune diseases. And this is getting worse. What *organic* nanotech can do is adapt existing medicines to tackle even these bacteria. Nanotech makes antibiotics, and a whole range of medicines, more effective.

Inorganic nanotech is a bit different. These are nanoparticles, usually either gold, magnetic metals or 'semiconductor quantum dots' (that's pretty sci-fi), which can imbue areas of our body with magnetic and electrical properties (yep, definitely sci-fi), making it much easier to scan for diseases and to tackle others. One frontier of nanomedicine is in cancer treatment. The tumour-targeting ability of nanoparticles enables doctors to scan for cancers more effectively, and allows scientists to design drugs that specifically attack cancer – as opposed to all cells, as chemo and radiotherapies do (see page 109).

But making medicines more effective and supercharging our immune systems are only the first steps in the exciting journey of nanotechnology. It's thought nanotech can also aid in recreating and repairing organs. Not only do nanoparticles direct tissue-healing drugs but they can also act to create 'biomimetic scaffolds' which mimic the structure of existing organs to guide and encourage natural regeneration.

We don't know how much we can do with nanotech. At the moment, it's simply used to make existing medical treatments better. But the future is hopeful. Nanotech could create stronger and lighter industrial materials. It could generate and store clean energy. It could even address pollution and climate change. Nanotechnology really is one of the best gateways humans have to a science-fiction future.

Society

If you believe a lot of modern evolutionists (as well as quite a few ancient scholars), humans are a naturally social species. We are pack animals who collaborate and communicate to our mutual benefit. Yet while we might be a naturally social species, that doesn't mean being social always comes easily to us – cities smell and other people are annoying. So we needed to invent a few things to make it all go smoothly ...

Society is all about those big ideas that have made living with each other just a little bit easier.

Human Migration
Bipedal Road Trips and Genocides

If you go back far enough, we're all East Africans. In fact, if you want to annoy someone, try calling up your local Tanzanian embassy to ask if you're eligible for a passport. I suspect they might argue that 150,000 years is a bit too far back. Because the first humans – and that means *all types* of humans – came from Africa. We know this partly because all of our closest evolutionary relatives – the bonobo, the chimpanzee and the gorilla – are most densely found here. But we know for sure because of all the fossil and genetic evidence we have.

What we don't know, however, is *why* humans first came down from the trees. My favourite hypothesis – the drunken monkey theory – is that our ancestral primates kept staying longer and longer on the forest bed because that's where the fermented fruit was. They just liked to get razzled.

Humans today – *Homo sapiens* – are only the latest in a string of 'human' species. The first two – *Australopithecus* and *Homo habilis* – didn't roam far from their African rainforest homes. That changed with *Homo erectus* with their itchy feet. *Homo erectus* had three things going for them that previous human species didn't. First, they were lean, strong and tall – their musculature was much more capable of lengthy journeys and painful endurance. Second, they could speak. The archaeological evidence we have shows that *Homo erectus* had the necessary larynx for talking. This, of course, allows collaboration and cooperation. Finally, essential for anyone wanting to leave balmy East Africa, they worked out how to make fire. Within only a few millennia, they had spread to most of Eurasia.

For one or two million years, you had a landmass dominated by *Homo erectus* and Neanderthals. Then, we come along, evolving from *Homo erectus*. For roughly 100,000 years, humans and Neanderthals lived side by side, but then (despite what you might think of your brother-in-law) Neanderthals died out. If you ever find yourself at a paleontological party (a wild affair), be careful what you say about this period. The debate is fierce. Some believe that *Homo sapiens* enslaved and killed Neanderthals. Others think it was all sharing and interbreeding until some third, unknown factor did for the Neanderthals. I'm not going to take sides, but what I will say is that wherever *Homo sapiens* fossils are found, you also find two things: a *lot* of knives and cutting stones (more than with other *Homo* fossils) and also a quick extinction of various other species.

The story of human migration is remarkable. Early humans built rafts and ships to get to Polynesian islands and Australia. They travelled for decades over freezing ice sheets to get to the Americas. They made homes in desert and tundra, swamps and mountains, on arid dust and fertile soil. The fact that prehistoric humans could, so quickly, populate the world with little more than sticks and stones is a story of which we should be proud.

Animal Husbandry
Man's Best Friend(s)

It's a cold night and you're sitting by the fire, desperately trying to get warm. Orth is bragging about his spear throw, and Tet's already snoring. You turn to get some food, and come face to face with a wolf. A huge, lean, slobbering, monster. You brace yourself and wait for the huge jaws to clamp down on your neck. But nothing happens. The wolf lies quietly nearby, gnawing on a shank bone. He's a companionable presence in the darkness, and he doesn't seem *that* scary any more.

One of the defining characteristics of *Homo sapiens* has been our ability to domesticate and tame animals. It's usually supposed that dogs were the first to be bred for their use in hunting, protection and eating our leftovers (like a prehistoric Roomba). But, even before the dog, recent evidence suggests snails might have been domesticated to be eaten as a reliable source of protein (they can be bred to be huge – as big as a human head in some cases. Which is lovely).

Roughly 12,000 years ago, in the Middle East, humans started to domesticate sheep and goats, and cows weren't too far behind. It took several millennia more, into around 4000 BCE and likely in the steppes of Eurasia, before we tamed the horse.

It goes without saying that animal husbandry rather changed things. Humans could now use oxen to pull ploughs, horses to travel great distances, eagles to hunt prey, dogs to scare off thieves and cats to destroy our favourite cushions. With domestication, we had milk, eggs and bacon to provide a more varied diet, wool to keep us warm and leather to protect our skin.

But it was not all a mooing and clucking idyll.

Firstly, living in such close proximity to large mammals meant that diseases could easily spread between species. Pathogens often find it hard to jump between radically different species (like from a rat to a human), but if they climb the ladder of rat to dog, to pig, to human, it's much easier.

Secondly, keeping animals requires a certain type of grassland. We're so used to our modern, cultivated countryside that we forget how *wild* land once was. Miles and miles of forests, huge floodplains, rocky mountain scree – these were the norm. It took a huge, millennia-long effort, across hundreds of generations, to deforest, irrigate, clear, drain and prepare the land for animals. Even today, about a third of all habitable land is used to keep livestock. The result is a great extinction – a damaging, depressing trend to biological monoculture. Land that was once exciting and diverse is now kept as grazing fields for cows.

But, even with these issues, animal husbandry was a turning point in human development. It allowed us to do more things, with greater efficiency. The edifice of civilisation was built on the backs of oxen.

Marriage
Legalising Sex

Immanuel Kant (1724–1804), one of the finest minds of the European Enlightenment, described marriage as 'the reciprocal use made by one person of the sexual organs and faculties of another'. Oddly enough, he never married. Yet although Kant's words are a long way from the romance of Disney movies, he was pretty much on the money – because for most of human history, marriage really was about legitimising sex and especially the children it (often) produces. It was a ticket to fornicate. A licence for lust.

Marriage goes back as far as written records allow. In ancient Babylon, more than 4,000 years ago, monogamous relationships were the norm and were bound by marital law. And those laws were predictably misogynistic. If a wife was caught cheating on her husband, both she and her lover would be drowned. If a husband did the same thing? It wasn't even considered adultery. (It's worth highlighting that marital rape is still legal in many countries, today.)

Before various religious authorities got involved, marriage was a peculiarly informal thing. Customs differed by locale, but it was pretty much the case that you only needed some kind of consent (or *family* consent) and a witness to get wed. If you'd had a few drinks, you'd best watch what you said – otherwise it was not impossible you'd end up married by the end of the night. Understandably, such casual arrangements were bound to end up in arguments – 'You can't marry her, she's my wife!' or 'Mate, she's your cousin; it's weird.'

In Europe, this was why the church stepped in. As society developed, people needed a third-party referee. So, slowly but surely, the Church took over what had previously been the remit of civil law.

But the idea that marriage was for love would have been an odd concept for our forebears (it still is for many cultures, today). Sure, it would be *nice* to have a loving marriage, and the idea of a devoted, romantic partner can be found in Plato, the Hindu Vedas, the French chivalric courts and the Romantic poets. But for most of history, marriage was about legitimising heirs or establishing a social welfare network called 'the household'. A husband or wife was the ultimate insurance policy for if (when) you got ill, out of work or old.

Nowadays, marriage is a lot of things, and can become strained because of that. We're told that marriage ought to be the source of all happiness. That if it lacks Kama Sutric sex and constant laughter, it's not a good partnership. But we forget how incredibly modern this idea is. For most humans who ever lived, and a good many in the world today, marriage is primarily a legal binding. It might not be the stuff of sonnets or Valentine's Day cards, but it's a promise, a commitment, and it's solid. And sometimes, that's just as important.

Cities

Unpacking the Suitcase

Your tribe has been moving around these mountains for many generations, as the Old Ones tell. Wherever the game and hunt take you, that's where you will go. It's a good, simple life. Ah, to be a nomad. Then one morning, Ur speaks up.

'I'm staying here,' he says. 'I like this river and I don't want to move.'

Ur's an idiot. He's never been good at hunting and spends far too much time with his plants. Green-fingered, lazy mud-lover. You're just about to hit him on the head when someone else speaks up.

'Good idea,' she says. Others join in. Ur stands on a big rock, beaming.

'So be it!' he says. 'I shall call this place Ur.'

You sigh. Ur's an idiot.

Although small villages and agrarian settlements had existed for thousands of years, new, organised and complex urban environments were something else. The first cities emerged in Mesopotamia (in modern-day Iraq) in the fourth millennia BCE but it wasn't long before others sprang up in Egypt, China and Mesoamerica.

For this to happen, there needed to be two big changes. First, a city required a trading system to feed and supply it. With so many people in such a small area, there was no way everyone could grow their own food. And so a city and countryside symbiosis was established. Second, a city needed a degree of planning that a simple communitarian tribal structure couldn't provide. To build walls, houses, roads, a marketplace, an economy and some kind of rudimentary sanitation system demanded a central organisation. It's no wonder, then, that with the rise of cities we see the rise of governments and empires (see page 136).

From the markets of Beijing to the agora of Athens, city-folk have identified themselves as different from their country cousins (and vice versa). In Roman times, people were either *Homo urbanus* or *Homo rusticus* – refined, genteel urbanites or boorish country bumpkins. Of course, today, such a division is as offensive as it is ignorant, but for a lot of history it wasn't far wrong. Because cities allowed *culture*. It's only when you have an economy of exchange that you can have societies that divide their labour. So tradesman can sell their tools to farmers, who sell their crops to nobles, who buy tickets at the theatre.

In his recent book *Sapiens*, Yuval Harari makes the compelling case that once humans started living in cities there was no going back. The sheer numbers of people living in cramped, urban societies couldn't go back to the peripatetic hunter-gatherer life. So, we continue to grow and continue to develop. But, with every new million people added to some city, we take a step away from our *Homo sapiens* roots (see page 126). The more we join the city, the more we become something else.

Nations and States

Passport Queues and War

There are few countries in the world that have never been colonised. Empires were the norm throughout most of history – the Americans were British, the British were Roman, and Romans were French at one point or another. The idea of a 'state', with inviolable borders and the right to self-determination, would have been laughable in much of the past. A land belonged to whoever claimed it and a people were subject to whoever conquered them.

We're so accustomed to 'nation-states' today – with our passports, colour-coded maps and Olympic Games – that we forget just how modern they are.

Although we often use the words interchangeably, a nation and a state are very different. A nation is more like what you'd call culture – it's about how you identify, where you feel at home and what your values are. A state is a geopolitical entity, with borders, laws and governments. Normally, a nation and state overlap, but that's not always the case. Before the creation of Israel, the Jews were a stateless nation. Inversely, most countries today are multinational states, which is to say that countries like Canada, Nigeria, Turkey or the UK have a *whole lot* of cultures living under one government.

Iceland and Japan are among the few places worldwide which have (mostly) one nation in one state. A post-colonial, globalised world of migration, economic interdependence and political cooperation makes this kind of cultural homogeny nearly impossible.

The geopolitical idea of the state is no less tricky to dissect. The idea of a citizen goes back to the ancient Greeks and was perfected by the Roman Empire. But, after 212 CE, the Emperor Caracalla made it possible for anyone to be a Roman citizen, regardless of their locale. Most political historians trace the modern state back to the Peace of Westphalia in 1648. In the run-up to this treaty, the Thirty Years War was devasting Germany. Lords, barons, dukes and anyone with a wall bigger than a fence declared themselves King of Wherever. It's thought around a third of the entire population of what is now Germany were killed in this period. When sanity was temporarily restored, everyone decided it was a good idea to establish a norm of territorial sovereignty – which is the principle of 'your country, your rules'.

Of course, a state's territorial sovereignty is hugely controversial. Not only do would-be emperors, dictators and global pariahs violate the principle all the time but there's also the messy issue of foreign intervention. The Nazi commanders who ended up at the Nuremberg Trials argued that the courts were illegal nonsense. What right did foreign powers have to tell them how they should make their laws? After all, nothing the Nazi Party did (at least domestically) was 'illegal' by the German laws of the time. But sometimes morality is bigger than sovereignty (see page 164). The idea of borders – a notion that goes back only 400 years – is hardly reason to abandon the concept of right and wrong.

Empires

When One Country Is Never Enough

When Sargon of Akkad (d. 2279 BCE) murdered his master and stole the throne, he found there were no more home-grown enemies to conquer. So he did what any teenager would do in that situation – he went off to murder his neighbours and steal all *their* stuff. With his victories, Sargon birthed the first empire – the Akkadian Empire. Their win was Syria's loss. And Turkey's loss. And Iran's loss.

Empires are a complicated and controversial area of history. On the one hand, they facilitate progress and their central hubs serve as scientific and philosophical melting pots. But it's progress that's almost always built on the back of slavery, exploitation and conquest.

When we talk of ancient civilisations, we're usually talking about empires. The Babylonians gave us one of the first known legal codes in the Code of Hammurabi (1750 BCE). The Egyptians gave us astronomy and advanced mathematics. The Chinese Han gave us paper, ceramics and the wheelbarrow. All empires, and all fertile grounds for science and culture.

But no empire quite matches the sheer ambition of the Romans. The reason the Roman Empire stands out in history is because of how it viewed integration. Thousands of roads crisscrossed the empire and huge engineering projects sprang up everywhere – all Roman designed and Roman built. Nowhere else in history had there been such a degree of economic and cultural assimilation. The legal and political systems of Western Europe and America are based on or inspired by the Roman model. The very notion of 'citizenship', born in ancient Greece, was popularised by Rome. Cicero's line *'Civis Romanus sum'* ('I am a Roman citizen') showed the power that came from being part of a supranational super-state. Where Rome differed from previous empires is in just how *Roman* it made its subjects. Every empire before Rome seems, by comparison, like a collection of rebellious, temporarily cowed, vassal states.

Today, geopolitics and international relations are almost entirely defined by the shadow of empire. The industrial and scientific revolutions that emerged from the British, French, Spanish and later American empires were at least partially catalysed only by exploiting the rest of the world. Some countries across Africa, Latin America and South-East Asia struggle today with poverty, corruption and internal conflict because they still live under artificial, desultory, uncaring bureaucracies originally forced upon them by empires that created extreme wealth disparities by exploiting them for resources and raw materials. Empires take and destroy, and parade a few choice innovations to justify their rapacity.

So, empires are a difficult chapter in our history books. They gave us railways, medicine and the global trade in goods, but they also gave us concentration camps, blood diamonds and slavery. A big idea, definitely, but one with a troubled legacy.

Structural Engineering
London Bridge Shouldn't Fall Down

As any runaway little piggy will tell you, building a house is easy but building a *good* house is much more difficult. The earliest humans built their structures – their houses, animal pens (see page 128) and religious monoliths – using whatever they could find around them. It might be baked mud in hot areas or stone and flint in wet ones. We've found evidence of small, wooden artificial islands (known as 'crannogs') as well as entire buildings made from mammoth bones. But these structures were never more than rudimentary. So long as they vaguely did their job, they were good enough.

If the human race were to build anything colossal or monumental, it would need structural engineering.

The word 'engineer' dates back to the Romans, whose industrious and indefatigable legions could build anything and everything. An 'engine' in Latin meant largely a 'war engine' – things like battering rams or ballistae. But a Roman engineer was also expected to also build roads, bridges, walls and open-air lavatories all over the empire (the latter being decidedly less enjoyable in Scotland than in Naples). Hence, an engineer.

For the tiny minority of readers who haven't built their own house, it might seem like a pretty straightforward thing – walls, floor, roof and 'we're hosting Christmas!' But not only is maintaining stability over time pretty hard, it's harder still when you throw in all the variable loads (or 'live loads') a structure has to bear. Your hobbyist house might survive a few pigeons on the roof, but throw in rain, wind and snow (10cm of snow over 1m^2 will weigh roughly 80kg) and you'd better be ready for some creaking.

Which is why most large ancient and pre-modern buildings had to have ridiculously large bases – like the pyramids at Giza (which were the tallest structures in the world for 3,000 years). A major step forward in structural engineering came with the humorously named flying buttresses. These allowed loads to be spread around to different parts of a structure – making it possible to build tall and beautiful Gothic cathedrals without a falling steeple killing the congregation.

But the biggest development necessary for modern engineering was reinforced concrete. Iron had been around for millennia, and iron bridges and monuments were common, but the idea of putting iron *into* concrete? That only became popular in the eighteenth century. Having extra-strong concrete now meant that skyscrapers and huge structures could be built. The Giza Pyramids were old news; now it's all about the Chrysler Building and Burj Khalifa (the tallest building in the world at time of writing, at 829.8m).

Today, we erect more buildings in a year than the Romans did in a century. Houses are bigger, more efficient and much more attractive than at any time in human history. And it's all down to concrete and people in hard hats.

Money

The Cause of, and Solution to, All Life's Problems

Imagine that, by some wizardry, there's suddenly no such thing as money. All of our banks, notes and numbers on screens are gone. How would you go about your life? Let's say you wanted to go on holiday. What would you offer the pilots, hoteliers or restaurateurs for their services? Imagine a world in which you have to trade a haircut in return for a rare-cooked steak.

We're all so used to money, so wired into an elaborate, inescapable financial architecture, that we forget just how transformative an idea it is.

There is nothing in this world that is inherently valuable. It is you, as a person, and we, as a society, that bestow this value. The first recognisable 'money' originated in Egypt and around the Fertile Crescent in the Middle East. These early examples were more like chits or ration vouchers: 'The bearer of this token is entitled to three bags of grain.' In fact, in the ancient world, granaries acted a bit like a bank – you deposited your grain and then withdrew what you wanted, when you wanted.

What's important about money is the 'pay the bearer' bit. If the writ or the currency names you specifically – 'pay Jonny Thomson' – then it can't be used in exchange. And exchange is what money is all about. Eventually there was no need for a written chit at all, as coins were invented to serve the same function.

The problem with money, though, is that it's only as good as the authority that supports it. If a regime collapses, who can you rely on to guarantee the worth of your cash? If a coin is stamped with the head of some deceased foreign despot, it seems pretty legitimate to say, 'Your money's no good here.' Most of us live in countries where we're lucky not to have to worry about this kind of thing. But those in Zimbabwe or North Korea will know the fear that all your savings today might be worthless tomorrow. It's why, throughout history, as today, people will 'buy' the most stable, guaranteed currency in the world – from Roman *denarii* to American dollars.

The Chinese were the first to clock the fact that lugging around chests of coins was tiring work. So they invented paper money (and paper too, actually). It became fashionable to leave coins with big, reputable shops, who in turn issued promissory notes – the equivalent of 'McDonald's owes the bearer ten boxes of copper'. This was then universalised under the Song Dynasty (960–1279).

Even if you're a kibbutz-living, hat-weaving, crop-growing off-gridder, it's hard to deny that money makes things a lot easier. I, for one, am glad I don't have to write a chapter of a book each time I want to buy some milk from the shops.

Banking
Can't Live with 'Em ...

I'm a reputable kind of guy. I write books and have little to no criminal history. I'm good for it. Will you give me your life savings to look after for a few years? Go on. I'll give you a fiver if you do.

You have to really trust someone to give them your money. But sometimes the alternative is worse. Before the time of banks or deposit boxes, you'd probably have a safe space in the house to put all your savings. Or maybe a hidden place you mark with an X on a treasure map for future generations to find. Both of which are pretty risky. How would you feel about heading off to the shops or going on holiday knowing that every penny you had was lying under that squeaky floorboard next to the boiler?

In the Code of Hammurabi – the oldest legal code we have from ancient Babylon – we can read about regulating interest rates. Banking, back then, involved private individuals giving loans at eye-watering rates. It meant a circling pool of loan sharks, not marble-lined foyers. The earliest 'banks' were probably granaries. Slaves and workers would not be given money but rather a chit that entitled them to a portion of grain (see page 140). The pyramids were built by cashless, zero-hours contractors.

Given both Christianity and Islam have strict rules about 'usury', it was left to Jewish populations to lend money or keep savings. Which meant that for most of history 'banker bashing' spilled over into outright antisemitism. In fact, Edward I of England even used the Jews' high interest rates as an excuse to execute and expel huge numbers of them in the thirteenth century.

Banks, as we know them today, owe their existence mostly to the Italian city states. Insanely wealthy families like the Cerchis, Bardis, de Medicis and Peruzzis set up banking houses in the major cities of northern Italy. In the relative security of a unified Holy Roman Empire, branches sprang up all over Europe. This was the time of the European empires (see page 136) and so the idea of banking was exported all over the world. All of the modern hallmarks of current banking were polished and fleshed out in cities like Genoa and Florence – things like savings, currency exchanges, issuing notes, loans and so on.

Bankers today, as in all history, are always the villains. It's easy to hate people who are both filthy rich and own 42 per cent of your house. For a lot of people, there's something a bit unpalatable about taking a huge cut of other people's hard-earned money. Yet without banks, the modern world would not exist. No venture or project could begin without credit, after all.

But if you really do hate bankers, I'll happily look after your savings for you.

Corporations
Nothing to Lose, Everything to Gain

Hiding in the back of a crowd feels safe. You can say, shout and do what you want, and it's highly unlikely you'll be found out. It allows you to be braver. There's not much that can stop the rolling swell of a mass of people. It's this fact that motivated the invention of the 'corporation'. As the eighteenth-century lawyer the first Baron Thurlow said, 'Corporations have neither bodies to be punished, nor souls to be condemned; they therefore do as they like.'

Corporations are what allow entrepreneurs to explore, innovate and experiment, and they transformed (possibly even gave birth to) the world of international finance.

Before corporations, a tradesperson was personally liable for any cock-ups. If the fence you built fell down in the first wind, if the shoes you cobbled had holes in them, or if the ale you brewed blinded people – you'd probably better hotfoot it out of town.

Corporations made business a bit more … safe. They worked (and still work) according to two main principles: a 'capital lock-in' system and 'limited liability'.

In traditional Roman law, commercial backers could essentially exit at will. They could take out their invested money whenever they liked. In the new corporation system, developed in the seventeenth century, investors had to keep their money in the companies until the end of a certain period. This meant these corporations could operate with a guaranteed pot of money (at least for a few years).

And, thanks to limited liability, they could use that money in far more adventurous and innovative ways than before. Limited liability simply means that a director or owner's personal assets are protected and ring-fenced from creditors. For example, if Jan gives Alex Incorporated £400 for an investment and Alex Incorporated loses it all, Jan can't go after Alex's private money to reclaim her losses.

The first demonstration of how useful a corporation could be involved European shipping companies – like the Dutch or English East India ones. Not only did these companies require vast start-up funds but they were risky business. Entire fleets would be wrecked, their crews would drown and their cargo would make some deep-sea fish very rich. Yet, thanks to the legal loopholes corporations enjoy, these companies could make a very handsome profit. So much so that they eventually became so large and rich that they rivalled even some nations in their strength.

With the dawn of the corporation, we entered a new age of finance – one of stock exchanges and shareholders. In the twenty-first century, almost all of the world's business is run through limited companies. Today, Walmart has a revenue that exceeds that of Belgium. And it's all down to the fact that no one gets blamed when things go wrong.

Mass Production
John the Pinhead Maker

My friend Joe is a DIY kind of guy. His weekends involve screws, drills and elbow grease. When I mentioned I was buying a shed, he said, 'Just YouTube it, mate. Do it yourself.' Joe is the kind of person who can build a shed. I, though, am the kind of person who views changing some batteries as a great engineering success. The point is that some people in life are Joes and some are not. We each have our specialities and skills.

It's this idea that lies behind the development of mass production.

Economies have specialised for a very long time. Since the first cities (see page 130), few humans have lived self-sufficiently. Instead they have taken up professions and traded for what they need. I'll swap my leather purse for your woollen blanket. He'll swap his fish for her medicines. But the idea of specialisation *within a single factory* only really came about in the eighteenth century.

In *The Wealth of Nations* (1776), the Scottish economist Adam Smith illustrated the 'division of labour' in the famous example of a pin factory. In the traditional method of manufacturing, one workman would make an entire pin – drawing out the wire, shaping it, cutting it, making the head, fitting the head and so on. (Never did you think you'd learn so much about pin production than in reading Adam Smith.) Smith's point is that this 'old way' of doing things is laborious and time-consuming. Different skills and tools are required for each job. But if you have one person doing only one job, you're much more productive. One person makes all the wire, one person cuts all the wire, and 'Here's John, he's the pinhead maker.'

Using the factory line, Smith claimed each worker could contribute to making '4,800 pins in a day' but alone 'they certainly could not each of them have made twenty, perhaps not one pin in a day'. Although these numbers are surely exaggerated, Smith was onto something – the division of labour and mass production were here.

In 1789, Eli Whitney invented the 'interchangeable part', making Smith's idea more efficient again. Whitney realised that if you made parts of the assembly line transferable you could reuse and repair them easily. So, for example, a musket might be made up of a certain two-inch tube, but so too could an organ pipe, or a whistle or a pistol.

Not much has changed with the factory line since the eighteenth century ... except the workers. Where, once, factories were made up of underpaid workers, they are now made up of unpaid robots. A robot will, unflinchingly and ceaselessly, make pins all day and all night. They don't need sleep or food, and they hardly ever unionise. And never mind pins; today, Foxconn's huge iPhone factory in Zhengzhou, China, can churn out *half a million* smartphones a day. Productive, yes, but so much supply and consumption does, somehow, feel just a little dystopian.

Trickle-down Economics
The Rising Tide Raises All Ships

The boss has arrived in his obscenely priced car, two hours after everyone else, wearing his bespoke suit.

'Good news, everyone,' he says. 'Profits are up!' He waits for applause. He's met with a smattering of grunts.

'Which means, I'm happy, the Board is happy and the *directors* are happy! But, most importantly, it means a 1 per cent increase to your salary.' Now that did get a few cheers.

'After all,' he finishes, 'what's good for the company is good for *everyone*.'

Welcome to trickle-down economics.

Trickle-down economics is the idea that the rich getting richer is good for the poorer in society as well, because wealth will 'trickle down' to them. When the rich have money, they invest it in their businesses, spend it on products and create jobs. More money in people's pockets means it gets spent somewhere, and this can only boost the economy and stimulate growth.

This idea was popularised in the 1970s by the economist Arthur Laffer, and governments still cite it today when setting tax rates. Laffer argued that, sometimes, if you increase the taxes on people, you actually take in *less* revenue overall. This is because people batten down the hatches and spend less. And spending less is bad for the economy. When you don't buy a new TV, that means a company has sold one less TV. And if a company's profits fall, they make salary cuts and redundancies, thus their employees have even less to spend. Inversely, when you *lower* taxes, there's more money in the economy, everyone buys enormous new TVs, and economists, everywhere, are happy.

Of course, if you lower taxes *too* much, you take in no revenue at all. The relationship is illustrated by the Laffer curve, a bell curve that highlights the Goldilocks point between too-high taxes on the one hand (where people stop spending) and too-low taxes on the other (where the government gets nothing).

Unfortunately, the success or otherwise of trickle-down economics is hard to determine. But 'Reaganomics' provides an interesting case study. In 1981, President Reagan introduced a range of deep tax cuts, hoping this would stimulate the economy. But it didn't – unemployment continued rising and inflation jumped to 20 per cent. Reagan had fallen off the Laffer curve. Over the next six years, taxes were slowly increased until they *did* hit a sweet spot. The US economy experienced a great boom in the later part of the 1980s.

... But an economy is complicated, and no one factor can account for growth. Yes, tax cuts might have helped, but so too did federal investment in motorways and defence. Or it might have been the deregulation policies or the boom in computing, telecommunications and biotechnology. As with all things economic, there are no easy answers.

The Welfare State
No One Left Behind

With the internet, globalisation and cheap international travel, we perhaps do not appreciate how important community used to be. For most of (post-nomadic) history, it would be rare for most people to stray more than a few miles from their home town. Today, that would be a bit weird. But back then your local area was not simply your home, it was your support system. A monastery or church would care for the poor, monks would take in the sick, and your family or neighbours would look after you as you got old. A community was responsible for everyone in it.

The earliest records we have from Babylon feature some attempt to provide for the poor. We know, too, that almost all holy books insist on charity. For instance, in Confucian philosophy, *yàoláo* is the basic ethical principle to care for the elderly and in Islam, *zakat* (charitable donation) is one of the 'five pillars'. Despite a lot of contrary evidence in this book, most humans are kind if they're given the opportunity. Caring for a hard-up friend is second nature.

The formal 'welfare state' is said to have started in the nineteenth century, but this glosses over a great many earlier welfare systems. The Egyptian vizier (a local governor) would organise provisions for the poor. The Roman 'grain dole' from the third century BCE was a grain handout to everyone, regardless of status (its occasional removal caused riots). In the Islamic caliphate, the Bayt al-Mal was a treasury explicitly ring-fenced for social welfare. And in Mesoamerica, both the Incas and Aztecs took in welfare taxes to distribute to those in need. The idea that welfare began with industrialisation is something of a myth – a myth that undersells human compassion.

But the nineteenth century was when reformers tried to systematise welfare. While individual countries differ in their details, most, today, offer variations on the 'Bismarck' model of social insurance. This is where an employee, employer and the state each contribute to a pot that then offers financial support to those who are ill, injured or retired. You pay in, in order to one day take out. Another system, the 'Beveridge' model, is where tax income provides certain provisions – such as healthcare – for *everyone*, no matter who, at no (or minimal) cost at the point of receipt.

Today, welfare is a contentious issue. Few will argue for its removal – after all, the test of a humane, civilised society is how it treats its worst-off. But there's one big issue: retirement. Retiring once meant you were infirm and unable to work. It was a euphemism for a few final peaceful years before death. Today, retirement means holidays and living the dream. And, if you have long retirements, you have long state pay-outs. There are no easy solutions to this, but perhaps one answer might be a return to the olden times – back to the days when your community was your responsibility and your neighbour deserved your care.

Advertising
The Top Three Hits on Google

You're sitting at your desk and in walks Lindsay, a spring in her step. She's humming, smiling and she's clearly desperate to tell you something. You sigh.

'What is it, Lindsay?'

'Smell me,' she says, and gives a wafting spin.

'Is that ... soap?!' Lindsay's smile gets wider.

'Uh-huh,' she nods. 'I saw that advert in the newspaper and it's *fantastic*. Here, I bought you some.'

It's hard to imagine a time when washing and soap were not ubiquitous. Once, washing too much was commonly seen as unhealthy – it was thought to open the pores to let in 'bad air' (see page 26) or, as one seventeenth-century French doctor said, 'It fills the head with vapours. It is the enemy of nerves and ligaments, which it loosens.' But within the course of a few years in the nineteenth century, that all changed. And it was all thanks to Thomas Barratt's Pears soap adverts. It's one of the earliest and most successful examples of an 'ad campaign', and it ushered in the era of modern advertising.

Advertising in some form is as old as commerce. It's impossible to imagine someone selling their wares without trying to make them seem more appealing. It might be a fruit seller screaming discount deals or a mural pointing towards your shop. In the ashes of Pompeii, we find both wooden signposts and hanging adverts.

But modern advertising – mainstream and mass produced – only came about after one key invention: Gutenberg's printing press (see page 244). Within only a few years, there were leaflets and flyers promoting local church meetings, magic tonics or a physician's prowess ('Only two people killed this month!'). When these presses became more efficient – and capable of printing large newspapers a few centuries later – they opened up even more possibilities. The first 'ad agencies' were set up in London in the early 1800s. People like William Tayler and James White worked out that they could place adverts for *national* products (made in the big cities) in *regional* newspapers and charge for the privilege of being the middlemen.

For almost all of history, advertising has walked in step with the evolution of media. The radio was invented, and twenty years later the first radio advert was sold (a whopping ten-minute-long one). The TV was invented, and a decade or so later, Bulova watches got the first TV ad. The 'golden era' of advertising – the *Mad Men* period between the 1960s and the 1980s – was an arms race of creativity, consumer psychology and copywriting genius.

Today, adverts are mostly digital. YouTube ads, sponsored posts on your timeline and the first few hits of your Google search are all, in some form, adverts. You are worth around $200 to Google and $750 to Amazon. Wherever you put your eyes, and whenever you click your mouse, someone is trying to sell you something.

Nudge Theory
The Whispers in Your Ear

A smart meter is a real-time energy tracker that tells you just how much energy you are using. It tells you in either kilowatts-per-hour or (my favourite) in cold, hard cash. When I first got one, I was obsessed by it. I would turn every appliance in the house on and off just to measure how much it was costing us. 'Babes, that kettle is costing us £10 an hour!' I'd shout, and 'Don't shower for too long!' Within a week, the smart meter was gone – banished to the hidden recesses of our boiler cupboard. The smart meter is an example of nudge theory (in my case, it's an example of a nudge too far ...). It's a small and discreet reminder which aims to change your behaviour for the better.

In the mid-2000s, the behavioural economist Richard Thaler and the law scholar Cass R. Sunstein first introduced the world to the idea of 'nudge psychology'. The idea behind it is that you establish with people a certain narrative or suggestion that will then influence their future behaviour. Often, it's a sense of communal or patriotic duty that's established. For instance, giving people 'I Voted' stickers or placing slogans like 'Keep America Beautiful' around green spaces are nudges designed to appeal to a sense of collective responsibility. But the 'nudge' could be any small change or law that is intended to have huge knock-on effects without the need for heavy-handed taxation or regulation.

A classic example of nudge theory is the 'checkout bag fee'. In 2002, Ireland introduced a 15-cent charge on plastic bags in shops. Not a bank-buster but mighty annoying. Before the charge was introduced, plastic-bag litter amounted to 5 per cent of all pollution. By 2015, it was 0.1 per cent. Similarly, when the UK introduced their 5p charge on plastic bags (largely donated to good causes), usage dropped by 97 per cent. It was great for the environment, great for charity revenues and great fun to watch proud idiots carrying armfuls of shopping half a mile to their car when they'd forgotten their tote bag.

Nudge is, essentially, a very clever form of advertising. Its job is to get inside the heads of consumers and manipulate them with their own biases. A good nudge should not *limit* the choices of people being nudged – people *could* still not vote and Ireland's shoppers *could* still get a bag. What's more, Thaler and Sunstein believed nudging should only ever be used for the good of the nudgee. For example, a nudge like listing calorie information on restaurant menus is intended to improve our lifestyle. My smart meter was intended to reduce my energy use.

Nudging is not without controversy. Some people call it manipulation and others call it 'nanny state' interventionism. But without a doubt it has become one of the most powerful, and successful, ideas in the history of marketing and consumer psychology.

Mutually Assured Destruction
I'm Taking You with Me

There's a tiny, single-celled marine animal with a ridiculous defence mechanism. If some roaming predator comes across the dinoflagellate, they'll glow continuously. They'll glow so brightly as to attract another, bigger, predator – a predator so big that it will eat them both. The result is that predators in the area know not to mess with the dinoflagellate because, frankly, it's insane. Why try to eat an animal which is willing to bring down predatorial fury on everyone, taking itself with you? Better to eat a bit of seaweed, or something.

It's a ridiculous idea, and it's one we've all depended upon for seventy years.

The nuclear bomb changed warfare. Suddenly, one nation had the power to level an entire city. Whole armies would be turned to dust in a mushroom cloud. The USA first discovered the atomic bomb, and used it to terrible effect against Japan, but for many years it wasn't the game changer it's seen to be today. Not only were there very few bombs available but also the delivery system (B-29 bomber planes) had limited range. So, it was unlikely, for example, that the Truman administration could have defeated the USSR in 1945 by using atomic bombs.

In any case, within four years the Soviet Union had developed their own nuclear weapons. For the first time in history, two rivals – two countries with bitterly opposed worldviews – had the means to obliterate the other. To counter this, the Americans developed a policy of 'overkill' – or nuclear superiority. Deterrence, under Eisenhower, meant maintaining an overwhelming imbalance of power, so that even if the Soviets used one or two weapons, the West could return the destruction a hundred times over.

The problem, though, was that the USSR didn't stop at one or two but increased their nuclear capacity much faster than the US anticipated. In response, between the 1950s and 60s, the Americans increased their arsenal by 150 per cent, and the power of the weapons doubled – the bombs of the late 1960s were more destructive than those used at Hiroshima and Nagasaki combined.

At first, the Kennedy government publicly adopted a 'city avoidance' policy – they'd attack only Soviet military or strategic settings, if it ever came to it. However, the USSR were conspicuously unwilling to commit to a like-for-like policy, so the US eventually adopted the fully apocalyptic policy of Mutually Assured Destruction (with never a truer acronym).

Today, we live in a MAD world. If any nuclear state chooses a 'first strike', then they, too, will be annihilated. While we no longer live in the heady Cold War days of imminent Armageddon, it's still disturbing to think that humanity's existence hangs on the rationality of just five heads of (nuclear) states. Given our long, terrifying history of being *irrational*, it's enough to keep you up at night.

Politics

If you put two people into any given room, you get politics. Because politics is all about power. Who holds it, who should hold it and who should never, ever be let near it. Anyone who's been subjected to a 'Right, everyone, get into groups!' activity will know that power is, most often, necessary. Someone needs to take charge if something is to get done. But if there's one thing the history of politics tells us, it's that everyone has a different idea of how things should be run – and that can lead to conflict.

Politics is about power and how to distribute it.

Monarchy

Heavy Is the Crown,
But Heavier Are the Chains

In the Disney film *The Lion King*, we are introduced to the happy world of monarchy. Mufasa, overlord of the savannah, rules his subjects with a beneficent but undoubtedly sharp paw. The gazelles and the elephants, the meerkats and the warthogs all bow to the might of the leonine dynasty. It's a world of blue-blooded rulers and prostrated herd beasts, all in the 'Circle of Life'. There's no meritocracy here – as Mufasa reminds his son, 'Everything the light touches will be yours.' The giraffes' grazing areas, the termites' hard-built mounds and the monkeys' arboreal homes – they all belong to some far-off monarch, a king they hardly ever see.

To a lot of the modern world, the idea of monarchy is peculiar. Why is it that one bloodline has immediate right to rule over everyone else? What makes a prince a better leader than you or me? And yet it's probably the first and most basic form of government we have had.

The first time a chieftain, warlord or local bigwig puts on a crown, they become a monarch. In fact, there are so many *types* of monarchies – absolute, representative, elected, hereditary and so on – that it's probably best to define it simply as a 'strong leader' system. The general idea is that monarchies invest power or sovereignty (see page 164) in a single person. In a hereditary system (the most common, historically), when the monarch dies, this power passes to the next in the bloodline.

Often, these royal dynasties will legitimise themselves by the use of historical precedents ('my forebears beat back our hated enemies!'), divine right ('God Himself has made me king!') or outlandish mythological origin stories. In the UK, monarchs have traced their line back to the legends of King Arthur. In ancient Ireland, the monarchs' regal forebears supposedly drank from the cauldron of the high god Lugh, endowing them with sovereign power. Ethiopian emperors were said to be descended from the union of King Solomon and the Queen of Sheba. The Aztec emperors owed their origin to the celestial tumbling of the Sun and Moon.

In a pre-industrial age, with disconnected communities and agrarian societies, monarchies were stable, practical and effective. They helped to appoint and manage powerful bureaucracies, and acted as a cultural focal point, around which people could come together. In many ways, they're the reason nations exist at all.

But with so much power vested in one individual, a monarchy's success inevitably depends on personalities. With a Queen Elizabeth I, Qin Shi Huang or Darius the Great, a state will flourish. With a Caligula, Ibrahim the Mad or Nebuchadnezzar II, things look decidedly, homicidally, worse. Today, the general political trend is that it's probably best to spread the power about a bit.

Church vs. State

Don't Talk About God at Dinner

Come on, mate, there's a time and a place for religion, isn't there? You don't bring it up at a polite dinner party. What you do on Sunday is up to you, but don't ram it down my throat!

This idea – the idea that religion belongs only in religious spaces at designated times – is an anomalous affectation of modernity. It's also one which belongs largely to the Western intellectual tradition.

Plato, like his master, Socrates, did not have much time for religion. Or, if he did, he certainly didn't think you should talk much about it. Plato believed that religion was a personal matter, to be kept, ideally, inside your head. As he wrote in his book *The Laws*, 'The gods are not to be brought into any public or private meeting.' Augustine – probably one of the most influential church fathers – took on a lot of Plato's ideas, and he developed the idea of church-state separation. In his great work, *The City of God*, Augustine lays out two types of kingdom: the earthly City of Man and the divine City of God. The City of Man is one of greed, egoism and vice. The City of God glorifies all that is good, altruistic and virtuous.

In some respects, we even owe the idea of 'secular', meaning 'set apart from religion', to Augustine. The word secular once meant the span of a human life, and this is why Augustine used it to contrast with the perfection of God. A *saeculum* was transitory and finite. God was constant and eternal. So, thanks to Augustine, medieval church dogma established the rule: humans do human things; God does Godly things. Of course, this allowed the Christian Church to stand *apart* from worldly courts. This meant that kings and emperors, regardless of their power, were always subordinate to God's law (and God's vessel, the Pope). It's this belief that likely influenced the ideas of rule of law and human rights which took root so firmly in Christian countries.

From the eighteenth century onwards – in the age of revolutions and nation-creation – we get constitutions written with a church-state separation in mind. In America, the first Amendment declares: 'Congress shall make no law respecting an establishment of religion, or prohibiting the free exercise thereof.' In Revolutionary France, the church was so vilified that churches were rebranded as 'Temples of Reason' and a deistic 'Cult of the Supreme Being' was established. Today, no modern democracy forces their citizens to believe a certain way (although it rarely pays to be seen as atheistic – especially in America).

The separation of church and state is important. It gives freedoms to our political institutions that might otherwise be hamstrung by blasphemy laws or a thought police. It allows people to debate ethical and legal issues without requiring the input of reference to millennia-old texts. It gives power to the people and not to the clergy.

Sovereignty
You Hold No Power Here

The idea of a state's 'sovereignty' is as contentious as it is important. At first glance, it seems such an obvious idea – it's the power of an authority over a territory. But how does this align with modern concepts like globalisation and interconnectedness? The notion of what and who is sovereign and how far the jurisdiction of that power extends has become a popular, and elusive, point of discussion.

The question, 'where does power lie?' goes back at least to antiquity. In the generation or so that saw a transition in power from the Roman Republic (and their Senate) to an Imperator (Augustus), philosophers tried to pin the concept down. But one of the best (if not the first) to articulate a coherent account of sovereignty was the sixteenth-century French legal scholar Jean Bodin. It was perhaps hardly surprising that it was during the anarchy of France's Thirty Years War, where rival and competing claimants to power ripped the country to bits, that Bodin felt the need to define how authority should work.

According to Bodin, a sovereign authority must be 'the absolute and perpetual power of a commonwealth'. This is to say, a sovereign power must have nothing superior to it, and it must be stable and fixed. A sovereign state has responsibilities to other states, but no one and nothing can ultimately *tell* it what to do.

Of course, Bodin was writing in an era of seemingly apocalyptic death and violence, so his ideas of sovereignty were an attempt to re-establish and secure the need for order. The idea that we, the people, the body of a nation, have absolute power and sovereignty came a little later, with Thomas Hobbes (1588–1679). Hobbes believed that when a people sign over their power to some other higher authority (a monarch, a senate, an oligarchy – whatever), they do so forever. You can't go back from that contract. While we've broken with the irrevocable contract bit these days, we still live with the Hobbesian idea that our governments exist by *our* grace. *We* are the ones who have true sovereignty, and the government only governs because we say so.

Bodin, and thinkers in the early modern period more broadly, believed that sovereignty was absolute and the highest authority on earth. But how does that work in today's interconnected world? Any international trade, diplomatic or military agreement requires compromise by both parties. Is being part of NATO a violation of sovereignty if members must contribute money to it? Are international criminal courts a violation of a state's sovereign right to do as it will?

Though it seems an obvious idea, it only takes the slightest picking apart to have the concept of sovereignty cascade into a torrent of problems.

Aristocracy
Good Stock and Blue Blood

Etymologically, there's little difference between a meritocracy and an aristocracy. But in reality, there's a universe of difference. *Aristos,* in Greek, means 'the best' or 'the most fitting' – so if we have an aristocracy, where the *aristos* are in power, then technically that means we are being run by the best (a meritocracy). And yet this is not how we generally understand aristocracy. For many people, aristocrats are supercilious, patronising, undeserving snobs. They're an antiquated relic of a crueller past.

But, however uneasily the concept sits in many modern states, the notion of an aristocracy has deep roots across most cultures.

The twentieth-century French philosopher and anthropologist Claude Lévi-Strauss believed that all humans, everywhere, have one predictable characteristic: we create an 'us' and a 'them'. We divide the world into binaries all the time – citizens and foreigners; adults and children; aristocrats and *hoi polloi*. Britain is notoriously obsessed with 'class', but most nations have a version of it – whether defined by wealth, status or birth. If we believe Lévi-Strauss, it's our nature to fragment and delineate.

It's hard to disagree with the historical evidence. In ancient Athens – the archetypal beacon of democracy – of the roughly 300,000 inhabitants, only 20,000 were actually allowed to vote. Women, children, slaves or foreigners couldn't get a look-in. The 'Golden Age' of Greek society was one dominated by the nobility – Pericles, Herodotus and Plato were all of good, elite stock. In the Roman Republic, supposedly another paragon of democracy, half the ruling consuls came from the same ten families. In the European medieval period – the age of chivalry and flowery insignia – an obvious blue-blood ideology was reinforced. The entire feudal system was built upon the idea of a monarch at the top and degrees of aristocracy all the way down to the peasant class. In China, up until recently, power was vested in a small group of shifting dynasties. In fact, in any complex society you find a form of aristocracy: the Mayans had the *ahau*; the Romans had the patricians; and the Maori have the *ariki*.

Ironically, though, however unfair and undemocratic the concept of a ruling elite is, their existence is what has historically paved the way for modern liberal democratic states. As an aristocracy gets more power or wealth, they demand more rights from the ultimate ruler (the monarch or emperor) – they gather together and they *demand* freedoms. Freedoms which will, eventually, trickle down to everyone (ideally). This is what happened with the Magna Carta in England, the Chou Dynasty in China and the Samurai in Japan.

It seems, then, that aristocracies are an historically unavoidable facet of complex societies, but they're also a socio-economic catalyst for change. For much of history, aristocrats were arrogant and condescending, but they also took on the even bigger, even worse tyrant above them.

Democracy
Give the People What They Want

Democracy must once have been thought a ridiculous idea. For centuries, society had been ruled by a tiny elite, trained to govern, their power passed down by birthright. And then someone thought it sensible to give *the people* a say. Plato, a witness to the earliest democracy in Athens, thought it was as stupid an idea as letting a crew captain a ship. What did *the people* know about government?

But the idea stuck, and it's turned out to be the richest, strongest and most innovative form of government in all human history.

We're so used to the concept of democracy that we often forget just how complex it is. In ancient Greece, democracies were 'direct', which means that those who could vote (which was a very limited section of society) could do so on pretty much every major issue. Going to war? Let's vote. Raising taxes? A vote. Opening a new school? Yep, let's vote. We talk about voter fatigue today but the Greeks would be laughing in their togas.

What we're most familiar with, today, is known as 'representative' democracy – where we vote for someone to do all these things for us. The idea is that these representatives (MPs, senators, delegates and so on) know better than the average Joe, and it frees us all up to get on with life. We elect these people, they gather in a parliament or a senate, and they debate and make laws.

Historically, the biggest issue surrounding democracy has been who makes up the 'demos', the people who get to vote. In Athens, it was only native-born men. In the Roman Republic, again, only men could vote, and your class and status also determined just how important your vote was. The crazy idea that *everyone* could vote only picked up steam in the nineteenth century. There was a variety of voter reform (suffrage) movements across the world, but the best known are the suffragette movement in the UK and the Seneca Falls Convention (1848) in the USA.

But if the history of the world teaches us anything, it's that those with power are reluctant to share it. It took the better part of a century, and a world war, for the US and UK to finally give women the vote in the 1920s – well after New Zealand, in 1893. It would take another few decades, and another world war, before the world's major democracies lowered the voting age to eighteen. Seen in context, democracy has actually existed in its current form for only about half a century – still a toddler, by world history standards.

Democracy is not a static thing. Like the governments that it throws up, the system itself is constantly changing and mutating. The question is: what will it look like tomorrow? And will it survive a world facing foreign intervention, cyber-attacks, media disinformation and artificial intelligence?

The Mechanics of the Modern State
Why Politics Should Be Boring

The definition of a dictator is someone who dictates whatever law they want. Most of the time, this is an awful idea. You get people like Rome's Caligula demanding that his horse be made consul, Haiti's Duvalier ordering all black dogs to be killed, or Libya's Gaddafi insisting all his bodyguards be young, attractive women. Having all the power vested in one person is bad news. It's why almost all democracies in the world – and all stable, modern states – have a version of the 'separation of powers'.

For a government to function, you need people who, separately, make the laws, enact the laws and interpret the laws – or, in the language of political theory 101, you need a legislature, an executive and a judiciary.

The legislature is the place where politicians and leaders write, debate and pass the laws of the land. The reason you can't steal, smash a window or drive on the wrong side of the road is because a government, somewhere, made that a law. We sometimes think of the police as the same thing as the law, but their powers are entirely restricted by an elected body.

The job of applying these laws falls to the executive. This is usually run by some head of state – a prime minister or a president, perhaps – and involves thousands of civil servants. The civil service goes back to ancient China, where parents would drill their kids to pass the imperial examination – a rigorous test of Confucian philosophy, literature, mathematics and current affairs. It was intended to be meritocratic – peasants and nobles alike could take on the lucrative role.

The third power of a modern state is the judiciary. The judiciary does not make or establish the law, it *interprets* it. Judges – especially the highest judges – have two roles. The first is to decide whether the facts of a certain case constitute a violation of a law or not. Their second role is to keep the other two powers in check. A legislature and an executive – if dominated by one party or a charismatic leader – could, in practice, take on a dictator's power. The judges have the final authority to stop any violations of sacrosanct laws, often spelled out in constitutions.

One thing missing from our modern discourse about politics is how *boring* it is. It's about long committee meetings, redrafting documents over and over again, and compromise. This is exactly as it's meant to be. Democracies move slowly, yes, but they move carefully. They might not be quick to respond to the winds of change, but they offer stability when the world is in flux.

Communism
A Marxist Tree

The word 'communism' is like a Rorschach inkblot – people will see their own biases in it. Is it the philosophical works of Marx? The Chinese monoculture of Mao? A cool image of Che Guevara on a T-shirt? Communism is not simply one thing – as with all philosophies, it's more like a tree, with twisting and knotting offshoots. And if Communism is the tree, then Karl Marx is the trunk. One with two huge branches: Leninism and Maoism.

In his *Communist Manifesto* (1848), Marx argued that capitalism would eventually and inevitably bloat on its own excess and collapse into a *global* communism, a world in which all property is owned communally and society becomes classless. So, let's grab the popcorn while we wait.

Lenin, coming to power in Russia in 1917, saw things differently. He was hugely influenced by both Marx and Engels but his ideas were couched firmly in Russian history, where he saw none of the tradition of democracy or liberalism that Marx wrote about. Instead, he called for a 'vanguard' to lead the communist revolution. This politically conscious intellectual elite would represent and lead the proletariat to throw off the chains of their oppressors. This was necessary, he felt, because in a country like Russia, the peasant and working-class population would not have the organisational or theoretical ability to take on the bourgeoisie, nor to run a socialist country. Where Marx saw inevitable change, Lenin saw the need for a short, sharp push.

Leninism largely collapsed with the Berlin Wall in 1989, but as Chairman Mao's postwar China proved, there was life in the communist tree yet. For Marx, the Communist revolution was not meant to happen in China or Russia. It was to happen in post-industrialised, late-stage capitalist countries like Germany, France and Britain. China, ravaged by the Second World War, and with an overwhelmingly agrarian economy, was a far cry from this. But nonetheless the Communist ideology took root as Maoism.

Philosophically, there are two major beliefs that differentiate Maoism from Marxism.

First, where Marx believed that history was an *economic* inevitability, Mao believed that *ideology* was the greater driver. A 'class struggle' for Mao did not need to be the factory workers vs. the owners but could exist *within* a class – or even within the heart of an individual.

Second, Marx saw the class struggle as coming to a utopic resolution – where the proletariat would establish a classless, peaceful communist society. Mao, though, believed that all things in life co-exist and are defined by their opposites. There was no resolution for Mao, instead there was permanent revolution and struggle.

Communism is complicated and, like all politics, its problems are glossed over by believers and exaggerated by opponents. But at its peak in the 1980s, around one-third of the world's population lived under communist states. It's probably fair to say that no political ideology has influenced the modern political landscape more than that Marxist tree trunk.

Fascism

How to Spot the Signs

Godwin's law states that the longer an internet discussion goes on, the more likely it is that someone or something will be compared to the Nazis. Why do Nazis dominate our popular mindset so much? Why did the obsession with fascism not end in 1945? Perhaps it's because fascism never really goes away – it hovers like a spectre at the fringes of society.

Fascism at its most basic is really just an extreme form of nationalism. It's a system of government that idolises and promotes national identity above all else. Through the use of propaganda, patriotism and opposition to this or that, a particular country is elevated to a quasi-religious status. It is the altar to which we all must bow. So, whilst fascism is often associated with certain charismatic leaders – Hitler, Mussolini, Franco – strictly speaking, it is only because they represent the national ideal. Your job, your family and even your life are all servants to the great nation.

Fascism is practically inseparable from the idea of totalitarianism – itself a term coined by the 'philosopher of fascism', Giovanni Gentile. This means that the government has *total* control over the political process, the state bureaucracy, the armed forces, the police and the secret police, the direction of the economy and, of course, the propagandistic mass media. The reason why fascism is such a modern idea is because of how it uses the media.

Fascistic propaganda has two hallmarks:

First, it tries to foment an oppositional attitude. It divides people into an overly simplistic 'us' and 'them'. The 'other' is almost always another racial group, and they must always be inferior to the good, native citizen. 'They' are subhuman, evil or traitorous somehow, and it's the job of a fascistic government to protect us from them and purge them from our society. This sense of superiority is what makes fascism different from regular nationalism or patriotism, which might emphasise difference and uniqueness without a value attached to that.

Second, fascistic propaganda appeals to the idea of resurrection. It speaks of an often-fictitious golden age, when everything you don't like about modernity didn't exist. Fascism imagines and hopes to (re)create some perfect society of ethnically or ideologically pure citizens, with just the right values. It wants to undo what it sees as the corrupting influence of consumerism, liberalism, homosexuality, atheism or any kind of impropriety. Fascists promise to make your country great again.

It's hard to be objective about fascism. It's an ideology of hate. It seeks to say a certain type of person is inferior, and it's a philosophy of violence and war. It's the belief system that lay behind the murder of 6 million people in the Holocaust. And while we might talk about Nazism a lot, it's not without good reason – there's a lesson to be learned. So that if, or when, we see fascism rearing its head again, we're better placed to resist it.

Liberty
It's Complicated

Despite what Mel Gibson, dressed in a kilt, might scream at us, 'freedom' is not an absolute good. It's simply not the case that more freedom results in a better society. For instance, I doubt any of us would want to live in a world where people are 'free' to murder, steal and assault at their leisure. What we call 'liberal' states today actually have a great many regulatory laws governing society and businesses. We don't let drunks drive cars or your next-door neighbour build a bomb. And yet, at the other end of the spectrum, too little freedom is the hallmark of totalitarianism and misery. The battle lines of politics, even today, are frequently based on what counts as 'too much' or 'too little' freedom.

For a lot of pre-modern history, liberty was understood not as an individual thing (the freedom you have to do what you want) but as a collective thing (something we all have as a political community). In the Greek city states and the Roman Republic, it meant having a say in how things were run. Freedom did not mean freedom *from* the state but freedom *to* direct it. Most often, this freedom meant democracy. It's this idea of freedom that motivated the eighteenth-century revolutionary movements in France and America. 'No taxation without representation!' shouted American revolutionaries. It's telling that the philosophers and scholars of these revolutions most often compared themselves to the Roman Republic or the Greeks. The Founding Father John Adams, for instance, would say the Americans were like the freedom-loving Athenians and compared the British to the tyrannical Persians.

Running parallel to this idea of democratic freedom was the concept of private freedom. Liberalism of this kind has often been thought of as an English tradition. The classic example is Magna Carta. This was the thirteenth-century document in which 'the people' (or rather, the rich barons) demanded rights for Englishmen. When, four centuries later, the English philosopher John Locke said the sovereign had no right over 'life, health, liberty and possessions', he was placing very definite parameters around the powers of a government (see page 170).

But it's disingenuous (and offensive) to assume no other culture considered liberty before the English. First, there's an argument that *Christianity* paved the way long before Magna Carta – with its emphasis on personal authority that allows only God as the supreme power over all. And, second, many non-Anglo thinkers wrote extensively about liberty, including Montaigne, Machiavelli, Rousseau, Aquinas, Augustine and Constant.

Today, 'liberal' has so many meanings as to be almost meaningless. It can describe the graffiti-painting motto of an anarchist as well as the voting behaviour of an elderly man in a cardigan. It can mean no regulations at all or a great many indeed. It can be political or social, economic or cultural. But however porous and flexible the term might be, the history of the world moves to the beat of 'liberalism'.

Free Speech

Sticks and Stones

If you so wanted, you could trash someone's life's work in print, slag off other people's opinions on the internet and heckle the Prime Minister – all because you live in a country where you have freedom of speech. The idea that people can voice an idea or say (mostly) what they want to (most) people without fear of repercussion is an old one, but that doesn't mean it's easy or clear-cut.

The ancient Athenian philosophers realised that if you cannot debate or challenge political ideas then there can be no democracy. How could rival politicians offer alternative visions of the future if they could only speak one version of it? The word *parrhesia*, or 'unrestrained speech', was a core value of Athenian democracy. Yet when the very same democracy sentenced Socrates to death for 'refusing to recognise the gods recognised by the state', it highlighted, in its infancy, the limitations of the idea.

While there are many examples of religious tolerance in non-European traditions (such as the Edicts of King Ashoka in India or in Genghis Khan's Mongolian Empire), there isn't the same strain of 'free speech' as found in the history of Europe. This strain owes itself to antiquity but also runs in tandem with a liberalism (see page 176) and an individualism that comes when you have a lot of very powerful lords all vying for control. A baron, duke or lord can say whatever they want if you haven't the power to stop them.

The Protestant Reformation gave a lot of power to the individual believer (so that, for instance, Papist stooges couldn't tell you what to say), and the Enlightenment's emphasis on human reason meant free debate and free discussion. One of the finest defences of free speech, even today, comes from the English philosopher J. S. Mill in the nineteenth century. He argued that free speech is necessary for three reasons:

First, it prevents you from being cocky (because someone might pick a hole in your position).

Second, it lends beliefs legitimacy or truth (only if we can attack a belief can we see if it holds).

Third, it keeps ideas from wilting into 'dead dogma'. Ideas such as liberty, democracy, honesty and civility need to be challenged, otherwise they grow dusty and forgotten. Without debate, we forget why a belief is important.

Today, no state has total free speech. You cannot share data that doesn't belong to you. You cannot shout state secrets. You cannot post bomb recipes on social media. Increasingly, many countries have laws that decree you cannot say anything 'hateful'. So, the Greek 'unrestrained speech' is not, nor has it ever been, realistic. But we do need freedom of debate and discussion. We need the right to protest, challenge and mock, as much as the right to defend and stand our ground. If you can't have multiple views, there really can be no democracy.

Human Rights

You Deserve Better

When the Second World War ended, the Allies had a problem. How were they to judge those informants, sympathisers and enablers who were 'only following orders'. After all, everything the Nazis had done – however reprehensible, immoral and inhumane – was, by the law of their land, 'legal'. Germans had been following German laws.

The problem the Nuremberg court found was that there was no international, universal law. Since the Peace of Westphalia (see page 135), most of the world had adopted a 'your country, your problem' policy. It was the era of turning a blind eye. But the world could not turn a blind eye to the Holocaust. Millions were murdered in the Final Solution, and as the Allies liberated Nazi-occupied countries, the depths of the horror were on full public display. The time had come for human rights.

The history of human rights is contentious. The notion of some kind of 'rights' likely goes back as far as the first legal codes. But, more concretely, some scholars cite ancient Greece and Rome as the birthplace of the idea. The Roman idea of *ius gentium* implies there was a natural law to the world – a 'law of nations' that every human was entitled to regardless of who they were. But it's hard to attribute the concept of human rights to cultures that enslaved entire peoples (see Civil Rights, page 186). There's little *ius gentium* about deeming barbarians, women and conquered people to be second-class citizens.

For human rights to be anything more than just words on the wind, they have to be enshrined in law. For that, we had to wait until the eighteenth century. The Founding Fathers of America were much taken with the English philosopher John Locke's ideas of 'natural rights', which led to Thomas Jefferson's famous line: 'We hold these truths to be self-evident, that all men are created equal, that they are endowed by their Creator with certain unalienable Rights.' A decade later, Revolutionary France followed suit, declaring, 'Men are born and remain free and equal in rights ... The aim of all political association is the preservation of the natural and imprescriptible rights of man.'

But these were local to certain countries. It wasn't until 1948 that the *Universal* Declaration of Human Rights was ratified by the United Nations (see page 182). And today, rights are still far from universal. Afghan girls cannot go to school, Rohingya Muslims are forcibly evicted from their homes and there are still more than 40 million slaves worldwide. But human rights are about more than simply laws and courts; they are about empowerment. In every oppressive dictatorship, in every windowless cell and in every abusive household people *know* their rights. They know they deserve and are entitled to better. Yes, human rights need better protection and enforcement, but the *idea* of universal rights? That's pretty big.

The United Nations

A New World Order

In international relations, the 'primacy of the state' is the idea that the supreme power and ultimate sovereign is the government of a country. A state can enter into treaties or agreements but can leave these any time they choose to – the state is supreme. Today, there are challenges to the primacy of the state. The biggest is that existential threats – such as international terrorism, people smuggling, weapons-dealing, global warming and the impact of technologies like AI – cannot be dealt with in isolation. No country can unilaterally resolve transnational problems. So we need an international body. A place for multilateral cooperation and pooled sovereignty.

We need a United Nations.

When a broken and exhausted populace surveyed the aftermath of the Second World War, they said, 'Never again.' Never again could the world allow a genocide to go unseen or an entire generation to be slaughtered in battle. With the invention of the atomic bomb, 'never again' became an existential necessity. Before the war, the formation of the League of Nations was supposed to have ended this kind of thing. It was set up in 1920 to be an international order that protected states and prevented war. Yet it was a toothless, underfunded organisation that no one took seriously.

After 1942, the Allies of the Second World War were called the 'United Nations'. When they formed the United Nations organisation in October 1945, they gave themselves the powers of 'permanent members'. These permanent members – China, France, Russia, the UK and the USA – can veto *any* decision the UN proposes. As you can imagine, given how dissimilar those countries are, it's rare to get them all aligned on anything remotely controversial.

The UN was founded to maintain peace and serve as a diplomatic arena where people could discuss things (hopefully) without escalating them. It played a major role in the Israel/Palestine partition (1947), mediated during the Cuban Missile Crisis (1962) and has been the principal driver of climate change resolutions such as Kyoto (1995) and Paris (2015).

In many ways, the UN has been supremely successful. Since its inception, there have been no world wars, no nuclear attacks, nor have any permanent members (openly) gone to war. The UN has the International Criminal Court to investigate human rights and to enforce the Geneva Convention – the internationally agreed 'rules of war'. Yet it doesn't take a political scientist to know the world is hardly all peace and harmony. The UN is often slow and bureaucratic. With 193 members, it's hard to agree on much. Its budget is just over $3 billion – which sounds like a lot but pales by comparison when you consider that the USA's foreign aid budget alone is $63 billion.

The UN might be a good forum, but without the driving will of its most powerful and wealthy members, it can offer very little. Perhaps states are, still, the most important players in international relations.

Feminism
Distribution of Power

In all historical and anthropological study, we have not found any compelling evidence for a *single* matriarchal society. We have a smattering of matrilineal societies (the Minangkabau of Western Sumatra, for instance, have property passed down the female line) and we have matrifocal cultures (the Iroquois respected women highly and gave them decision-making powers), but nowhere do we see women given meaningful *power*. Which means that, for most recorded human history, women have been led and controlled by men. Of course, we all know a handful of examples of great historical female rulers but these are exceptions that prove the rule.

Feminism is not an easy word to define, but we can broadly understand it as the idea that women ought to be given greater power, respect and recognition. This being true, it would be absurd to think there weren't feminists before modern times. But, as a *movement*, feminism began only recently, and is generally seen in terms of three 'waves'.

The first wave, mainly concerned with legal and political rights, is associated with names like Mary Wollstonecraft and the USA's Seneca Falls Convention. The second wave, with a focus on social and cultural injustices, is dominated by people like Simone de Beauvoir and Betty Friedan. The third wave is often considered a rejection or revision of the second wave and is concerned with what Kimberlé Crenshaw called 'intersectionality' – how feminism affects class, race, disability, etc.

Today, feminism is neither solely cultural nor political but both. Consider, for example, a big issue in feminist literature: the public/private sphere. What was certainly true in the 1960s, and is still true for much of the world today, is that the 'public sphere' – politics, work, economics and law – is dominated by men. The private sphere – domesticity and the family – involves women. Men are the political leaders and CEOs while women pick up kids from nursery and manage the home. The man leaves the house and interacts with colleagues – in *public*. The woman spends most of her day inside the same four walls, seeing only small groups of close friends, leaving the home only to 'pop out' for essentials.

The problem is the *worth* society places on each role. Worth is often defined by wages and success is measured by power. 'Unpaid labour' and 'stay-at-home mums' are labels with particular baggage. They're seen as less important and less financially valued.

The public/private sphere division is a microcosmic representation of gender issues more broadly, and the damage they cause. All the stereotypes and pressures of gender roles can destroy people. For men, constantly having to perform and live a life of public bravado is exhausting and can cause mental-health issues. For women, being excluded from the world outside can be lonely, depressing and limiting. Feminism is the attempt to make society better ... for *everyone*.

Civil Rights
Demanding What's Right

Every country's prejudices are different, and each has a unique history of oppression and complicated divisions. Take, for example, racism directed at black people. Here, Europe and the USA have a very different past. Both had slaves and both subjugated thousands. But, in the US, the African-American population lived and worked on American soil. As the writer Barrett Holmes Pitner puts it, 'There is no home country for African-Americans to connect to. Instead it is essentially a status quo of domestic alienation, dehumanisation, criminalisation, and terror.'

It's not as if, when slavery was abolished in the US with the 1865 Thirteenth Amendment, racism and exploitation ended overnight. Having a law against a thing cannot do away with over a century of oppression. A piece of paper, passed by a congress hundreds of miles away, could not overturn the deeply entrenched social, economic and political structures that sustained slavery across vast, distant tracts of America. Those structures still exist today.

The recognition of this fact was at the heart of the civil rights movement. The Jim Crow laws in the US South of the 1950s were deliberately designed to control black people socially and politically, and to exploit them economically.

After the Civil War, black people were forced into unskilled wage sectors and excluded from higher education and from management positions. Black and white people were segregated, with the former receiving far inferior services and facilities. What's more, black people were disenfranchised from the political process and had no legal means by which to challenge the laws which prejudiced against them.

Civil rights is a *movement*, involving a host of names whose brave battles for justice are largely lost to history books. And while characters like Malcolm X, Rosa Parks, James Baldwin and Angela Davis are shining lights of the struggle, there's one name that glows brightest of all: Martin Luther King, Jnr.

King was a vocal advocate of *nonviolent* protest. He thought that only nonviolence could 'seek to win friendship and understanding' and 'chooses love over hate'. But nonviolence is not to be confused with passivity. King rejected the 'do nothingism' that said black Americans should wait for change. Instead, he argued that protest should create a 'constructive tension necessary for growth'.

In King's 'Letter from Birmingham Jail', he takes aim at 'white moderates' who profess to be allies to the civil rights movement but then advise 'the Negro to wait for a "more convenient season".' He understood that 'freedom is never voluntarily given'. It must be demanded.

King's nonviolence was not always popular, and it's a debate still with us today – violent revolution or nonviolent protest? On the one hand, 'healthy discontent' might be seen as not enough to bring about substantive change. On the other, 'white moderates' are still at it, telling black people to tone down their activism. What can't be denied, though, is the courage, intelligence and spirit of Martin Luther King and the civil rights movement he led.

Environmentalism
The World's Broken

Environmentalism is a thing now. We sort our recycling and talk about 'sustainability'. The cultural zeitgeist has clocked the fact that something is broken in our attitude to the natural world. And we can see the damage everywhere: our countryside is less biodiverse, green spaces are shrinking, and every year since 1977 has been warmer than the average for the twentieth century.

Environmentalism – the social and political movement focused on protecting the natural world – came into the mainstream in the 1960s and 1970s, and it can be explored via one big name and one big idea.

The big name is Rachel Carson. Carson's *Silent Spring* (1962) was, principally, an attack on pesticides and harmful chemicals. It lamented the end of that background thrum of wildlife – bugs, birds and scratchy things – that only people over the age of fifty remember. She argued, 'Man's assaults upon the environment is the contamination of air, earth, rivers and sea with dangerous and even lethal materials.' But *Silent Spring* was about much more. It was about our attitude to the natural world.

The big idea comes to us from the Norwegian philosopher Arne Næss in 1973. Næss coined the term 'deep ecology' to refer to a realignment in how we see our place in nature. We are so used to seeing ourselves as the centre of the universe. Like some pre-Copernican astronomer (see page 64), we believe that everything exists in our orbit. Trees are there to be cut down or to look nice. Birds exist to delight us with their song. Bugs? Well, they're yucky, so who cares about them?

Yet this is all born of what Næss called 'human ignorance of biospherical relationships'. We see ourselves as the top of an ecological chain, not part of an interwoven, symbiotic system. As Næss puts it, 'The ecological self is not an isolated entity but a seamless part of the whole, with no clear boundary separating it from the environment.' Deep ecology is about reappraisal. Humans have no more inherent value than any living organism. We should not save the environment just to save ourselves; we should save it because it is a thing worth saving.

Næss' theory of deep ecology is radical and unpalatable to many. Owing to our evolutionary wiring as well as our religious and cultural traditions, it's hard *not* to see humans at the centre of things. Yet there's also wisdom in the idea that we are not the rulers of nature, only members of a community.

Environmentalism is often associated with obstructive protest movements, but it's much more than that. It's the awareness of the fact that we've gone too far. We've broken a relationship with the natural world and we're breaking nature itself – possibly irrevocably. Green politics historically polls poorly, and people switch off and bury their head when it's talked about, but it might just be the most important big idea in this book.

Utopia
The Power of Blue-sky Thinking

What would the perfect society look like to you? Try, if you can, to put aside how things are, or how you think they 'should be', and just imagine your own best possible world. What jobs would people do? Who would get paid the most or get the best houses? Would there even be money? Would there be any crime? Why not?

Sometimes a bit of utopian thinking is vitally important, and the very word (if not the idea) goes back to the sixteenth-century intellectual Thomas More.

More's book *Utopia* (1516) introduces a narrator who meets a traveller from the island of 'Utopia'. This Utopian tells us about a perfect society, free from any inequality and violence. A place with no property or unequal distribution of goods. Where jobs are divided fairly amongst the populace. In Utopia, violence is abhorred as the darkest taboo, and 'all men zealously pursue the good of the public'.

Yet there's a sinister aspect to this Utopia. If someone tries to leave the country, they are first imprisoned. If they try it again, they're made into slaves. All the streets are identical, and after ten years, everyone has to swap houses by lottery. All doors are open, and anyone can come and go as they please. Nothing is yours and nothing is mine.

Ask two scholars *why* More wrote *Utopia* and you'll get two different answers.

On the one hand, it's subversive and revolutionary. In a post-Marx world, it's impossible not to read *Utopia* without seeing the parallels with communism.

On the other hand, some see it as mocking and satirical. *Utopia* is *so* extreme at times as to seem an absurdity or a parody. The Utopian world is portrayed as overbearing and invasive, often at odds with human nature.

But even this interpretation, on its own, doesn't quite fit. *Utopia*, like all utopian ideas since, is a provocation. It's an open question to us, the reader, about how society *should* be ordered. It inverts everything we assume and asks how things could be different. It's a thought experiment.

Today, we live with the idea of utopias. We all have our own version. Is it one derived from science fiction, with humans living in distant galaxies? Is it based on nanotech and advanced AI (see pages 122 and 234)? Is it centred on a return to nature and respect for the environment? There are as many utopias as there are people.

Utopianism is the brave voice that challenges the status quo. But it's also the challenge that brings about change. Perhaps the best way to view utopia is like a rainbow. The closer we move to it, the further it moves away. And, while we'll never reach it, it's the idea of it that makes us all move forward.

War

Rarely the Last Resort

Despite this being a book about the greatest ideas of humanity, you may have noticed there's one depressingly familiar theme that pops up again and again - war. It's war that necessitates, funds and mass-produces some of the biggest technological leaps in history, from metallurgy to nuclear physics. It's war that establishes governments and develops political ideologies. The seventeenth-century English philosopher Thomas Hobbes even argued that the existence and threat of war is what leads us to have any society at all.

War is what brings out the worst in human history. It devastates continents and kills entire peoples. But it's also probably the single greatest catalyst for progress we have.

All the evidence we have tells us that humans are a belligerent species. Most pre-agricultural hunter-gatherer tribes were almost constantly at war, and it's thought 10–20 per cent of people could expect to die violently in these societies. With the advent of agriculture (see page 128), cities (see page 133) and empires (see page 136), things started to get safer, with your chances of violent death dropping to around 2–5 per cent. But large settlements and big stone walls only lasted for so long. Eventually, people figured out that horses could make raiding lucrative and successful. Fast-moving, unpredictable mounted attacks are what did for the Romans, the Jin and the Abbasid empires.

But from conflict great things can emerge; from ashes rises the phoenix. Throughout almost all history, when you find sustained, intense and frequent war, you find also great technological innovation, for good or ill. Motor vehicles, tinned foods (see page 199), radar, GPS (page 228), the internet (page 230), stirrups (page 208) and nuclear energy (page 82) were all either born of, or inspired by, war.

One example of this can be found in early modern Europe. Sixteenth-century Europe was divided into tiny, disconnected states almost constantly at each other's throats. Unlike the contemporary stable empires of China, Europe was a nightmare of bloodstained fields and burned-out villages. It was in this laboratory of broken landscapes that guns and cannon became a necessity. After all this intense military investment, within a century Europe's armies were the deadliest and best in all the world – and as a result, their empires would come to stretch over almost the entire globe.

But is war, as the Greek philosopher Heraclitus once wrote, really 'the father of all things'? War certainly does catalyse progress in some respects, but it can equally stifle it in others. Science and technology are invariably civilian developments; it's just their effects that are seen most obviously in war (such as the atomic bomb). Economic prosperity, stability and education are all necessary for progress. So beware anyone who tells you that war is *always*, in the end, a good thing.

War, like so many of the ideas in this book, is as complicated as the humans who wage it.

Technology

If you dare to suggest that humans are unique because of our use of technology, hold your breath and wait for the inevitable response: 'Actually, many animals can use technology.' Yes, crows use sticks to poke in holes and octopuses use clam shells as armour, but come on, it's not the same, is it? Humans have flown to the moon. We've split the atom. We've invented penicillin, electricity and the Slinky (the big three). Yes, other animals can use tools and make technology, but humans have transformed the world with it.

Technology is all about the ways humans have made the world work for us (and, sometimes, broken it in the process).

Irrigation
Artificial Rivers

Once humans stopped roaming and decided to *grow* their food, growing it well became a matter of life and death. For nomadic peoples, if the hunt is poor in one valley, you can hop over to the next. For settlers (see page 128), if your crops fail one year, you go very hungry. One of the earliest and most basic methods of ensuring a good crop is irrigation, the practice by which people build canals and waterways to nourish their farms. Over time, green-fingered innovators have given us exciting new ways to water crops, culminating in the *pièce de resistance*: the garden sprinkler.

In modern Egypt, around 95 per cent of its 110 million people live clustered close to the Nile's floodplain. Looking at a satellite image of the area is a great way to appreciate just how important being near water is. It's no surprise, then, that ancient pharaohs would store water in oases during dry spells, and they built complicated channels connecting the Nile with farms miles away. Around the same time, the Nubians developed (and the Persians perfected) the first waterwheel – a rotating wheel of buckets, turned by oxen (or people), which lifted water from a well and then into an irrigation tube.

While most people are familiar with huge Greek and Roman aqueducts, these look like child's play when compared with what hydraulic engineers were constructing in China around the same time. Chinese inventors devised a system of chain pumps, powered by animals, which could take water from a source at ground level to higher elevations. From here, gravity would funnel the water whichever way a local administrator chose – a marvel of ancient engineering.

It took a millennium before anyone could match such ingenuity with the windpump. Like their milling cousins, a windpump has a base fitted with vanes or turbines (depending on the era). Spinning, these power a piston which can draw water from a well far more efficiently than any previous method, irrigating thousands of acres a day. In the centuries after their invention, there was a great population boost wherever they were taken up. Better access to water means better crops, which means more food for all. The handpump, the smaller, cheaper descendent of the windpump, came along in the fifteenth century, bringing easy water extraction to the masses.

Irrigation is, today, a geopolitical hot potato. The reason Tibet – the 'Water Tower of Asia' – is so strategically important is that its high and abundant reservoirs are essential for irrigating a host of countries. Without Tibet's water, a great many Chinese farmers would find their fields arid within a year. Likewise, Ethiopia's control over the lower parts of the Nile is a threat to Egypt. If Ethiopia dam the river to produce electricity (as they are doing), it risks starving millions of Egyptians. Irrigation remains a matter of life and death even today.

Food Preservation

Smoke, Salt and Spam

Earlier this year, I think I went temporarily insane. I'd spent too much time reading the news – cover-to-cover stories about wars, catastrophes and 'disruptions in the supply chain' – and I indulged in what can only be described as 'prepper' behaviour. I researched what foods would last the longest and I bought an embarrassing quantity of them. I bought dried things and airtight things. I got pickled this and salted that. I had to find space for a *lot* of tins.

Nowadays, we are used to seeing aisles groaning with fresh fruit and vegetables when we go to the supermarket. But for much of history, this would have been an unthinkable luxury. Food needed to keep. It had to last a long winter, a bad harvest or weeks of travel.

The earliest examples we have of 'food preservation' involved heat. When the first pyromaniacs invented fire, it wasn't long before they realised that cooked stuff lasts longer than uncooked. What's more, whether by accident or design, they discovered that if you leave some meat hanging in a very smoky environment (in a time before functioning chimneys, this was pretty much everywhere) then it becomes both yummy and long-lasting.

While smoking was good, it was also onerous and only works for certain things. The next big food-preserving discovery was salt. Up until the eighteenth century, food preservation for armies and travellers involved a lot of it. Salt was so important to the Romans that some suggest the word 'salary' derived from 'salt-money'. Curing with salt works by reducing a food's water content. It's water that allows microbes to grow and reactions to happen. Reduce the water, and you reduce the chance of putrefaction.

Then, around 1795, the world was gifted the invention of a Frenchman, Nicolas Appert, aka 'the father of canning'. Appert put a variety of foods into an airtight glass jar and then dunked it into boiling water for long enough to kill the bacteria inside. Napoleon, a big fan of long marches, awarded Appert a special prize for his discovery. Within a decade or so, the Brit Peter Durand patented the use of tins instead of glass jars, and so began a long and exciting history of tinned tuna, tinned potatoes and Spam.

The mainstream way of preserving food these days is refrigeration. Snow-dwelling peoples had long noticed the effects of freezing their fish, but it was only when the American inventor Ollie Evans gave us the fridge that everyone could bring a little bit of Inuit into the kitchen. Today, we 'flash freeze' things (a method Clarence Birdseye popularised), we vacuum seal and we even use ionising radiation to kill nasties.

Food preservation is one of the many underappreciated conveniences explored in this book. It's kept millions alive and is what will see me and my food hoard through the upcoming apocalypse.

Navigation
Land Ho!

When you leave your phone behind, or when the signal stubbornly refuses to play ball, you quickly realise how easy it is to get lost. It's bad enough in an unfamiliar city, with landmarks, signs and people to ask. It's worse if you get lost in the wild, with its identical trees and squirrels that mock you. But imagine just how hard it would be to find your way when all you could see, from your nose to the horizon, was flat, twinkly blue. Imagine being on a ship, with pickled fish, limited drinkable water and no technology whatsoever, and deciding to just sail into the distance. How brave must those first sailors have been to set off from the shore for the first time.

This is precisely why navigation was so important in the history of mankind.

Luckily for us earthlings, wherever we go there's always *one* recognisable landmark to take our bearings from: the sun. The earliest sailors used the stars and the sun's position to tell them where to go. For instance, when you measure how far the sun or certain celestial bodies (such as the North Star in the northern hemisphere) are above the horizon, you can vaguely work out your ship's latitude (its north/south position). Longitude (east/west) is a touch trickier – you have to check the location of a star at the same time each day – and working out when to do this before there were clocks was, of course, no easy thing. But overall, so long as you have a clear night and a few good astronomical minds aboard, navigating by the stars and the sun isn't actually that hard. Stars will move as the Earth rotates, and you, too, will move. But if you know where stars lie in relation to each other, you can make pretty good estimates as to your direction.

We don't entirely know when humans first learned astronavigation. The oldest example (we think) comes from Polynesia – where sailors used the stars (as well as bird migratory patterns) to travel the thousands of miles around their islands. But it's likely to be older even than records can prove. When *Homo sapiens* first emerged out of Africa (see page 126) and spread all over the world, they would have had to cross miles and miles of deep, deadly water from South-East Asia to get to Australia. Yet 65,000 years ago they did just that. Of course, it might have been desperate luck, but for a species that had spent its entire existence migrating, it's more likely that they knew how to navigate very well.

Navigation was perfected by the compass and better maps (see page 202) but humans had been sailing great distances for millennia before that. Few, today, would be able to travel days, weeks and months on featureless, flat waterways, and many people are not even able to tell north from south. But then, why would they? We have our phones for that.

Maps

Representing the World

In many ways, reading a map is like going to the movies – we unthinkingly ignore the medium to focus on the message behind it. We do not see the screen; we see the story it tells. Likewise, a map lures us in by promising to be an objective and truthful window to the world, but it's much better to see maps as a *narrative* rather than a snapshot of reality. They are more works of art than schematics, each bound to a particular cultural history and designed with an aim in mind.

The earliest cave art that we have found dates back at least 40,000 years, and we started writing around 5,000 years ago (see page 242). So, you'd expect maps to come along pretty soon after. The problem, though, is that maps are hard for archaeologists to identify (with their unrealistic proportions and random squiggles) and many might be lost to history. So, the first maps where we can definitely say, 'Yes, that's a map' only appear in Babylon, around the sixth century BCE. Of course, that's a heck of a long time after the discovery of writing that humans decided maps were a good idea – probably because a mostly local-bound people had little need for them.

All maps are orientated to the needs of the user. The Romans weren't keen on maps (tourists, generals and travellers almost certainly didn't use them), but those that do survive place the Mediterranean at the centre ('Mediterranean' literally means 'middle of the world') with all roads leading to Rome. Chinese maps often involved gridlines, but the scale and projections used for them varied in different locations. Nicolas Visscher's seventeenth-century map of the Netherlands is lined with ideological statements about the powers of each region. The Dogon people of Mali almost always included celestial markers on their maps (such as showing the direction of the sun's travel to orientate east-west). The London Underground map is about train stations and not, strictly, an accurate account of London geography. All of these are maps, but all speak to the cartographers' underlying motives or preoccupations as much as what they actually represent.

A good map, broadly speaking, needs to do two things: first, it needs to provide a correlation with the 'real world' and, second, it needs either to help us understand it better or aid us in some other way. It's this latter, utilitarian aspect that is often overlooked. Consider, for example, the sat nav you use in your car. It's deliberately stripped bare of all topographical irrelevancies. No painted monsters or marginalia here. It's just about roads, routes and traffic. Its concern is journey time alone. An Uber driver's sat nav will be similar, but will also highlight pockets of supply and demand – where best to go to get more clients. The data is woven into the map.

The way you imagine your environment is almost certainly defined by maps. They not only prevent navigators from getting lost, they also define how you think about the world.

The Wheel
The Archetypal Big Idea

In 2022, a debate ignited across social media. It asked, 'Are there more doors or wheels in the world?' Each camp had its defenders and big names. Organisations like the BBC and NBC dragged out experts and specialists to give their answer. What the debate revealed is just how ubiquitous – and how necessary – the wheel is to our life. It's almost unfathomable how a society functioned without it.

It's true of most inventions, but after the fact, it seems ridiculous that there was a time before people had 'thought up' the wheel. It's so obvious, isn't it? So *useful*.

Wheels don't really exist in nature. You get beetles pushing balls of dung, and certain bacteria that (kind of) move by rotating, but these aren't wheels as we understand them. For a wheel to be a wheel it needs to be round and it needs an axle. The first wheel emerged around 3500 BCE, and what's odd, archeologically speaking, is that they suddenly appeared all over the place. It's one of those weird moments in ancient history when an idea seems to have shot around the world.

Before the wheel, people used a 'roller and sledge' method to move things about. This involved placing a heavy load on some kind of roller (like a log) and heaving it along. People would then move the displaced log at the back all the way to the front again. It was exhausting work, but at least it got your henges built.

Then, some bright, overworked builder spent a bit of time around potters. Potters were using something like a wheel to rotate their clay in order to make perfectly round jars and ceramics. The lightbulb moment came in realising how this could work just as well on a wagon or a cart. Suddenly, a single person could carry a load over distances that would have taken ten men ten days. What's strange, though, is that after this it took another 3,000 years for the wheelbarrow to be invented, in either ancient Greece or China (it depends which scholar you ask … if you can tear them away from the wheels vs. doors debate).

There's a myth that native American populations didn't know the wheel before Europeans arrived. They did have wheels – they were used in toys and pottery – but because they didn't have any great beasts of burden in the Americas (like horses or oxen), they were never used for wagons. The wheel, so instrumental and important to Eurasian agriculture, transport and development, was little more than a child's plaything in the Americas.

The wheel remained largely unchanged across history until the discovery of pneumatics and rubber, and even then it was simply modified rather than reinvented. It's all testament to just how much impact an *idea* can have. The wheel is so simple, so fundamental to our society, that it's hard to imagine a time when people didn't know what it was.

Swords
Smelting a Keen Cut

Sticks and stones will, most certainly, break your bones. For tens of thousands of years, that's exactly what they did. The first weapons archaeologists have found are stone-tipped arrows or spears, whopping great clubs and axes cut from the bones of some mammoth animal (if not the actual mammoth). What's conspicuously absent in the misty far-back time is the sword. It's hard to make an edge in nature, and if it's pokey power you want, an arrow or spear is much the better option. This all changes when some early, inventive metallurgists work out how to make bronze.

Most metals aren't that good for weapons. Gold and silver are easy to forge, but they're rare and they dent far too quickly. Tin is good for pots and pans but it won't hold up against that huge bloke with his tree-stump club. What you need is the earliest alloy known to history: bronze.

Bronze is the combination of copper and tin (mostly), although you can mix in other stuff to change the strength or ductility. The irritating thing for ancient weaponsmiths was that the tin and copper ores are rarely found together. A lot of countries today have deposits of both, but in the ancient world – a landscape of tiny, bickering kingdoms – having both was rare. This meant that possessing either made you a very valuable trading partner –

or an appealing invasion opportunity. Cyprus was the copper mine of the ancient Greeks and King Solomon made his (and ancient Israel's) fortune from his copper mines. One theory as to the etymology of 'Britain' is that it's derived from the Phoenician name 'Baratanac', meaning 'Land of Tin'.

Bronze is stronger than iron, but it's also fiddly and hard to work, which is why the Bronze Age gave way to the Iron. As with the wheel (see page 204), the discovery of ironworking pops up almost simultaneously around the world. (I'm not giving credence to 'alien technology' theories but it *is* weird how often this happens.) Ironworking requires extracting iron ore, having heat and furnaces to smelt it and Herculean shoulders to bash it into shape. But it was still much easier to manipulate than bronze. It made swords and armour, but it also made doors, railings and toys. Steel – iron's stronger and higher-status cousin – was not unknown in the ancient world but it was uncommon, especially in Western Eurasia. There are documented cases of ancient steelworking cultures – such as the Chinese, and the Persians with their 'Damascus Steel' – but it wasn't really until the late Middle Ages that steel became a proper industry.

For most of human history, we stabbed each other with long, metal things. They were even used during the Second World War (mainly by an under-industrialised, desperate China against the gun-carrying Japanese). Today, swords are usually ornamental or recreational – katanas or *gladii* hanging over the fireplace. After all, it's a silly person who brings a knife to a gun fight.

Stirrups

Giddy Up!

A lot of the ideas in this book are *big*. Writing, the wheel, gunpowder and nuclear weapons are obvious and famous leaps in human development. Few people, though, will imagine that two pieces of metal dangling from a saddle could be as important. Nor that it would take so long to think of them.

Horses were domesticated about 6,000 years ago, and there's a lot of evidence that they played a central role in most aspects of Eurasian life. They could get you around, plough your field and let you hunt across long distances. So, given how ubiquitous and useful a horse was, it's a peculiar fact that the saddle wasn't invented until around 800 BCE. That means there were 3,000 years of horse-hair chafing and sore inner thighs.

The problem with horses (as anyone who's galloped on one will know) is that it's pretty hard to multitask if you're on horseback. And that's *with* stirrups. Even accounting for the fact that people in previous civilisations would devote lifetimes to learning horsemanship, there's a limit to what you can do on a horse without them. As with the wheel and the wheelbarrow (see page 205), it beggars belief that it took another half a millennium from the saddle for some Chinese equestrian to realise two small appendages would be useful. With stirrups, riders could sit more comfortably and have more control over the horse. This opened up the possibility of horse racing, horse shows and leisure rides. But let's be honest: what it mainly did was allow people to kill each other more easily.

If you have ever been to a big event and walked past a mounted police officer, you'll appreciate the vast and terrifying presence of a horse. Now imagine a few hundred of those, armoured and decorated with insignia, each carrying a metal-clad knight holding aloft his ten-foot spear – and they're charging at you. Imagine thousands of Mongolian archers as they hoot and jeer, galloping around you. The European knights, the Arabic cavalry and the Steppes' horse archers all dominated and defined warfare in their time. They couldn't have done it without the stirrup.

The stirrup changed warfare and so it changed society. Armies no longer wasted time with plodding infantry taking months to arrive anywhere. They were all about shock charges, quick withdrawals and equine blitzkrieg. Battles were won and lost faster than ever before, and empires brought down at the pace of a charge. The Mongols, for example – the ultimate masters of the horse and stirrup – defeated both the Jin (in Northern China) and the Khwārezm (Turko-Persian) dynasties within ten years in the thirteenth century.

That's quite an impact for two humble strips of leather and a couple of metal arches.

Gunpowder
Pretty and Deadly

There are few ideas in this book quite as destructive as gunpowder. We've always been an aggressive, greedy, warmongering species, but with the invention of gunpowder, we could take murdering each other to the next level. It's a great irony, then, that gunpowder was actually first discovered by Chinese chemists looking for immortality. In old Chinese, gunpowder was called 'fire medicine' and was intended to cure mild fungal infections and rashes. It was the magic powder used by wandering physicians or for showy theatricals.

But something that burns and explodes easily was never going to stay obscure for long. As often is the case (see The Internet, page 230), when the army gets hold of an idea, that idea gets going.

There's a rather quaint myth that the Chinese were only using gunpowder for fireworks until the Europeans turned it into a weapon of war. In fact, within a few decades of gunpowder first appearing, the Chinese had developed flamethrowers and 'rocket' launchers (spears and chemicals fired from bamboo cylinders). But there is an element of truth to the myth. Because while there's evidence of Chinese cannons from the thirteenth century, it wasn't until centuries later that Europeans *refined* gunpowder to make destructive weapons of war.

Guns (using gunpowder) required two major developments. The first was something called 'corned powder', with larger granules that burned faster and was much more powerful. The second involved developments in metallurgy. Christian Europe had a healthy metalcasting industry making bells for churches and cathedrals. The casters often found easy (and better paid) employment making cannon strong enough to withstand the powerful blasts of corned powder. So, a double irony, then – gunpowder was invented to cure diseases and then turned into a weapon of mass destruction by people working for a religion that preached love.

From there, cannons were locked in an arms race against masons. A big cannon needs a big wall; bigger cannons need massive walls. Eventually gunpowder won out, and by around the eighteenth century, castles were no longer worth the money.

Today, gunpowder is made obsolete by its cleaner, cheaper, more dangerous cousin – 'smokeless powder' or 'nitro powder' (see Explosives, page 48). Gunpowder is an incredible example of how inventions get repurposed, and then refined across continents and generations (a bit like the printing press, see page 244). It's also a depressing testament to the fact that if there's a new way to kill someone, it's going to go mainstream soon enough.

The Clock

Slaves to Time

'Okay, Stu, tonight's the night. We're going to rob Baron Brown of all his treasure. Let's meet at the chapel when the evening star touches the horizon.'

'Sure thing, boss,' Stu replies. 'But ... err ... it's pretty cloudy tonight. Where's the evening star?'

'Good point. Okay, okay, let's meet at the chapel when this sand timer runs out.'

'Great idea, boss. Err ... So, who gets the sand timer?'

'Hmm. Bother. Okay, so when the bells strike four times, we'll meet then.'

'Do you mean the chapel bells, the baron's bells or the seminary's bells, boss?'

Keeping the time has not always been easy. While 'clocks' go back as far as ancient Egypt, at least, they were pretty loose with actual timekeeping. Sundials, water clocks and sand timers were good for vague timings, but each has massive shortcomings (like needing the sun or requiring constant refilling). Up until the late Middle Ages, this kind of 'that'll do' approach was enough. No one was really clock-watching, so long as the work was done and the harvest brought in. Most people would expect to work daylight hours – long, sixteen-hour days in summer, eight hours in winter. But as we moved into the machine era, this wouldn't suffice for the efficiency-driven industrialists of Europe.

The problem with clocks was that everyone had their own version. People in Town A would operate from the church's bell – one strike every fifteen minutes. People in Town B would use the local bigwig's fancy new pendulum clock (perfected by the physicist Christiaan Huygens in 1656). People in Town C would follow the ancient way of the sundial. Pocket watches had been around since the sixteenth century but they were luxury items and not coordinated with each other. It made inter-regional business impossible.

And inter-regional business was kind of the entire point of the postal service. So, in Britain – Europe's leading industrial nation in the 1800s – the Royal Mail service insisted that every guard on their mailcoaches carry a timepiece programmed to the most accurate observatory in the country: Greenwich. Hence, Greenwich Mean Time – the first attempt in history to synchronise time throughout different communities. The railways came next (after all, it's quite important to know when a huge, steam-spouting train is going to be coming along the tracks). In 1840, Great Western Railway became the first company to operate solely according to GMT. By 1855, 95 per cent of *all* public clocks were GMT-aligned.

Most technologies in this book were designed to fit the way we live or to make our life easier. Clocks are a curious exception. Clocks don't fit into our lives, *we* fit into the clock's life. We go to sleep at 'bedtime', not necessarily because we're tired. We eat at 'lunchtime', not always because we're hungry. We go to work because they're the hours we're obliged to keep. In many ways, clocks have not liberated us; they've enslaved us.

Steam Power

Choo-Choo!

If you've come to this entry after a few others, you'll have discovered that there's rarely such a thing as a 'revolutionary inventor'. The history of ideas is not so much about individual genius as amalgamation. Often, once you have the brilliant discovery of something, you get a lot of waiting around until *another* invention comes along to make the original discovery soar. So, we'd had flying gizmos for centuries but needed the combustion engine to make an aeroplane. We had moveable type for ages but needed fine metals to make the printing press. Great revolutions in technology come about when many conditions come together. Which is exactly what you get with the steam engine.

For the invention of the steam engine, we needed two other conditions to be met.

The first was technological. When you first learn about the steam engine, you wonder why it took humans several millennia to discover it. We have found archaeological remains of metal kettles from the earliest Mesopotamian cities, so we obviously knew how to create eruptions of steam. What the ancient peoples didn't have, though, were efficient pressure vessels. To funnel steam with enough precision and power to move things (like the rods on a train's wheel), you need to collect it in a high-pressure container. But when we're talking about these kinds of pressures, you need very high-quality metals. This, in turn, requires highly skilled metalworking. And that only really comes about in the eighteenth century, along with industrialisation.

The second synchronous condition necessary for steam power was socio-economic. The Romans, for instance, had no financial or logistic incentive to invent steam power. Slaves were cheap and in easy supply, and horses were perfectly sufficient for all your empire-creating needs. Up to the 1600s, there was simply no need for a steam engine – human and animal power did the job just fine. From the seventeenth century, though, there were two big, industrialising problems. First, humans couldn't get water out from mines that efficiently, and so we needed the steam pump. Second, horses couldn't move heavy goods around that easily. Roads were often slapdash things, literally cobbled together. They were only one wagon of coal away from a quagmire. So we needed the railway, and so we needed the steam engine.

The steam engine is incredibly simple when you break it down. You use fuel to heat a fire box which turns water in a pressure boiler to steam. This steam is funnelled to pistons which turn rods on the wheels to get them moving forward. The steam engine and steam power, then, is not so much a case of genius inventions as inventors filling a gap. It's only when society gives us a certain problem that we find a brilliant way to solve it.

Electricity
Modern Magic

'It don't exist, pal,' the gruff sailor says, as you step from the boat. 'You might as well look for Atlantis or Heracles' bow.'

You thank the man politely, but inwardly you mutter curses. You're here to find the Stone of Miletus. According to legend, the Stone is a glowing, amber gem that fizzles with power. When you put it near clothes, it'll fray them. When you put it near hair, it'll make it stand on end. The philosophers even say the stone is *animate*. Stupid sailor, what does he know?

The ancient world and history books are full of stories about things which sound a lot like electricity – lightning, obviously, but also electric eels, Chinese bioluminescent bugs or amber. The 'Stone of Miletus' was amber, and was known for its static electricity. The word 'electricity' stems from the Greek word for amber – *electron*. Even today, there's something undeniably magical about electricity. What is it if not dark sorcery, when you can press a switch and an entire room is lit up? How is using a remote control any different to a spell?

Every atom in the universe has the potential to create electricity, because they each have an electron with a negative charge. The reason the world doesn't suffer a constant celestial explosion of lightning is because atoms are, usually, balanced; the negative electrons are balanced by the positive protons in the nucleus (see page 80). Sometimes, though, when atoms rub up against each other, they transfer electrons to each other. In the process, one atom becomes a bit more negative and the other becomes a bit more positive. The result? Electricity. Rubbing up against someone can be, as John Travolta knows, electrifying.

The history of electricity, then, is a case of working out which atoms (when in contact) produce the best static energy and how best to channel that energy. After a lot of experimentation, electric shocks and fried circuit boards, we know that metals are good conductors of electricity. Others – like rubber or wood – are poor.

One of the biggest names in the discovery of electricity is the Italian physicist Alessandro Volta, who, in 1800, invented the battery. The Voltaic pile (which sounds like he needed a doctor) involves layers of zinc and copper, separated by sodden, brackish cardboard. Volta's battery could produce a steady flow of electricity and was the first historical domino flick that would lead to our modern iPhone batteries.

Electricity changed the world. It powered the Industrial Revolution and inspired Mary Shelley to write *Frankenstein*. It's hard to imagine now, but before electricity, people most often just went to bed when it got dark. You could use candles, yes, but for most people, across most of history, these were too expensive. Today, almost every aspect of life requires electricity of some kind. It's what gave the world both literal and metaphoric light.

Computers
No Going Back

It's because of pushy parenting that we have computers. Blaise Pascal – a child prodigy who was intensively educated by his single father – invented his calculator in 1642 to help his father reorganise the tax structure of Lower Normandy. All computers, then and since, have existed to serve a purpose. They make some tasks easier or allow us to do things we once couldn't. While the future of AI might change things (see page 234), computers are *tools* to plug the holes in our fumbling, bumbling human inadequacies.

Up until the 1930s, all 'computers' were basically calculators. Even the 'father of computers', Charles Babbage (1791–1871), was only trying to make it easier to calculate astronomical tables for the Royal Navy. Babbage did have great plans for a more 'general purpose' computer but sadly a breakdown and then his death conspired to get in the way. His dream fell to the polymathic mind of Ada Lovelace (1815–1852).

Lovelace first recognised that the algorithms a computer used did not have to be limited to star charts or calculations. They could create music, images and text. Lovelace is called the first 'computer programmer' because she recognised that there needed to be a *language* for computers. For instance, if we turned musical notes or letters into numbers, then Babbage's analytical engine would be only the beginning of what a computer could potentially do.

Lovelace was largely ignored in her day – she was both a woman and a century ahead of her time – but it was this ability to analyse *letters* that would herald the Computer Age. During the Second World War, the British codebreakers at Bletchley Park (headed by Alan Turing) developed first the Bombe and then Colossus to help break German communication codes (using the genius of Poles who had broken the Enigma code). Back then, computers were gargantuan. I doubt you have a room in your house big enough to hold a wartime computer.

The *personal* computer (PC) revolution was born with the invention of the 'integrated circuit'. The story is one of convergent engineering – where two teams, working largely independently of each other, both stumbled on something like the microchip. Robert Noyce, who would later cofound Intel (today, the largest semiconductor manufacturer in the world), was working on a silicon-based circuit. A rival, Jack Kilby of Texas Instruments, was working on a model which had a thin layer of semiconductor material grafted onto a substrate. Both inventions were brilliant. Both were revolutionary. But Noyce's was cheaper and easier to make, and that is what won the day.

The integrated circuit reduced a roomful of computer to something the size of a fingernail, and today, the $600 billion semiconductor industry underpins the whole world. Almost all the technology of the future needs a semiconductor – phones, cars, military systems, clean energy and, of course, computers. Which, when you think about it, gives a *lot* of power to the small number of semiconductor manufacturers worldwide.

Telephones

Ahoy!

Every time you say 'hello', you are picking sides in a 200-year-old culture war. When the telephone started to become popular all over the developed world, there were two early pioneers: Thomas Edison (American) and Alexander Graham Bell (Scottish). Graham Bell thought the nautical 'Ahoy!' would be a good way to start a conversation. Edison thought it should be 'Hello!'

The Americans won.

What this reveals is just how transformative an invention the telephone was. It wasn't only a new way of communicating, it was a new way of connecting. For all of human history, you could only talk to those near you. With the new-fangled steam transport (see page 214) you could get to others much more quickly, but for most people, communication still depended on written messages – either by letter or telegraph.

This changed quite dramatically at the end of the nineteenth century. Graham Bell's mother was partially deaf, and he used to talk very closely to her head so she could hear the vibrations of his voice. Unsurprisingly, then, Graham Bell devoted his life to studying the science of voice, acoustics and hearing. In 1863, Graham Bell read a book about how sounds could be transmitted by magnets and electricity using vibrating metal filaments. Thirteen years later, after tinkering with those filaments, he discovered that he could send a *voice* over this system. Within months he used the local telegraph line to talk to his father eight miles away. Within the year he was testing it over hundreds of miles. In 1876, Graham Bell got his patent – which is likely the only reason we actually know his name. There were over 600 legal challenges to his patent, three of which went as high as the US Supreme Court. He was not the only one experimenting in telephonics, it seems. But it was Graham Bell's patent that was upheld.

After 1876, the telephone became such an obviously useful asset that governments and businesses were falling over themselves to expand their telephone networks. In 1877, Thomas Edison improved on Graham Bell's transmitter to make voices clearer and louder (not the previous spooky, crackly shadow-voices of the underworld). In fact, this 'carbon microphone' was so good that it nearly bankrupted the Bell Telephone Company. Telephone exchanges came along in 1881, and by the turn of the twentieth century calls were being made from New York to London.

When you think about it, today, it's all bordering on sorcery. How can we turn my vocal sounds into waves that can be sent and reproduced perfectly across the world (or even the galaxy)?

These days, phones rarely do any phoning. The first mobile phones of the 1970s used wireless technology to make calls, but with the first text messages being sent in 1992 and then the iPhone in 2007, 'phone' became a catch-all term for 'entertaining communication device'. But it's still worth remembering how extraordinary it is to be able to chat to someone on the other side of the planet.

Radio
DJs and White Noise

The story of radio is not so much about invention as the accretion of learning. The Italian Guglielmo Marconi (1874–1937) is the one credited with inventing the radio, but that's only because he was the one who nabbed the patent. It could equally have been Michael Faraday, Hans Christian Ørsted, James Clerk Maxwell, Heinrich Hertz, Oliver Lodge, David Hughes, Jagadish Chandra Bose or Nikola Tesla who ended up with all the glory.

In the early nineteenth century, it was discovered that a current-carrying wire could move a compass needle located quite far away – over the air, as if by magic. When Michael Faraday found out that you could create *different* currents using different magnetic fields, an idea was born – messages could be transported 'in the air'. Over the course of the nineteenth century, inventors like Nikola Tesla developed more sophisticated and much more efficient methods of producing electromagnetic radiation, while Jagadish Chandra Bose and others worked out how to direct those currents reliably. The technology and science were all there. The scene was set for the big reveal. Enter Marconi.

Marconi was a great engineer in his own right and his big contribution to the invention of radio was in improving the length of the transmission – up to roughly two miles. But Marconi's real genius lay in his commercial mind. He founded a company in 1897, and by the next year he had shown that he could send radio messages even over the Atlantic. This was a huge moment in the history of communication. People didn't even know you could transmit radio waves over water, let alone that far. Backers were soon lining up to fund him. Mostly, Marconi's radio was marketed for shipping transmissions; it was his 'wireless telegraph' that sent the distress signals from the *Titanic*. This, in turn, was what normalised its use at sea.

After Marconi's breakthrough, the story of radio is one of refinement rather than reinvention. The early versions could only send out waves in short bursts – so they were only really good for signals or Morse code. In 1906, Reginald Fessenden gave us a generator capable of continuous waves, and the first 'broadcast' went live that year. (The term 'broadcast' is an agricultural term describing how a farmer would widely scatter their seed.) Two years later, a Frenchman on his honeymoon broadcast music from the Eiffel Tower, becoming the first DJ in history. And in 1974, the first radio signal was sent into space, for any aliens that might be listening.

According to the UN, there are roughly 44,000 radio stations today, broadcasting to 5 billion people. That's 70 per cent of the world's population, making radio more popular than the internet or TV. It's how a lot of the world still get their news, and it's how soldiers, police, and children camped in back gardens, communicate with each other. It's a rare example of nineteenth-century technology still being relevant today.

Flight
The Sky's the Limit

Your brother Wilbur gives you that irritating grin he always gives. For some unfathomable reason, the girls swoon over it, but right now, it makes you want to punch him in the face.

'Goggles on, brother!' he screams.

In your head runs a familiar script: *This shouldn't work. It won't work. Heavy things do not fly. We're not birds. We're not balloons – I'm just an idiot who's going to die.*

You're lying horizontal, strapped to the wing, as Wilbur starts the engine. The machine stutters and shakes. The sand from the windswept dunes kicks up into your face. You move forward slowly, then a bit faster, and then faster still. *Yep, definitely going to die.*

'Now!' screams Wilbur in your ear, running by your side. You yank your control and hesitantly, erratically, the *Wright Flyer* becomes the first manned, powered and controlled heavier-than-air vehicle to fly. Even if it was only for twelve seconds.

It is 1903. Overnight, Orville and Wilbur Wright become household names and they represent the breaking of a dam. Within sixty years, humans would be flying into space.

Humans have long wanted to fly. You can imagine some bored prehistoric boy looking at the graceful flight of a swallow and thinking, with a sigh, *Oh to be so free* (but in Neanderthalic grunts). And most historic attempts to fly have tried, to some extent, to mirror the mechanics of a bird. After all, what nature has made, humans can copy. But other than in Greek myths, not much success was had. While Leonardo da Vinci famously developed the schematics for a helicopter-like device, he hadn't the technology to create it.

The first flying humans emerged in the nineteenth century with Sir George Cayley's hang-gliders. The Chinese had invented kites several millennia earlier, but Cayley had the physics to turn them into flying machines. Ever the altruist, rather than take all the fame, Cayley let his coachman take the first human flight – with only 'very high' chances of death, and 'almost certain' chances of disfigurement. In my opinion, the hang-glider is one of the coolest inventions in the world, and I still don't know why we don't all hang-glide around the place all the time.

With the creation and then the improvement of the combustion engine (see page 50), inventors around the world were essentially in a race to be the first to invent a form of motorised glider. France, Russia and Britain all had pioneers in aeronautics, but history doesn't remember the losers – it remembers the Wright Brothers.

Space Exploration
Showing Off My Big Rocket

It took Christopher Columbus a long time to get backing for his 'other way round the world' idea. The Spanish eventually took a punt but, unfortunately, when he got to the 'New World' (*sic*), it was decidedly average. A few spices, silver mines and some pretty landscapes – not exactly the El Dorado he'd promised Spain. So Columbus did what any successful entrepreneur would: he lied. He said there were infinite beds of pearls, mountains of gold and bounties of cinnamon and pepper.

Because, as Columbus knew well, if you want money for something, you need an incentive. Few patrons will back exploration for the sake of it. It's this fact that underpins the astronomical advances in the twentieth-century's space race.

The reason humans looked to the stars was not for minerals or faster trading routes but for *prestige*. The USA and the USSR were locked in an ideological, chest-puffing, braggadocio war, where both were desperate to show the world that *their* way was the best way. A sure-fire proof was to spend millions on venturing into outer space. Because the Space Race was essentially about vanity. It was about showing the world who had the best manufacturing capacity and the best scientific institutions. It was all about who had the biggest rocket.

The Soviets shot off to a brilliant start. They put up the first satellite, *Sputnik 1* in 1957, followed by the first person in space, Yuri Gagarin, four years later. But soon the Americans caught up and, in 1969, Neil Armstrong became the first person to walk on the moon. From then on, the US kept a healthy lead. Being able to research and build space rocketry is expensive, and with corruption, stagnant productivity and deflated oil prices in the 1980s, the Soviets just didn't have a strong enough economy to keep up.

Space exploration is a hard and resource-heavy business. It needs rocketry, obviously, but also spacesuits, life-support systems and radiation shielding. NASA's recent Artemis programme is estimated to cost just under $100 billion by 2025. That's the same as the entire annual GDP of Slovakia.

So, is it worth the effort? In some ways, yes. The discoveries we've made from space travel are monumental. We've observed cosmic radiation to validate the Big Bang (see page 84), discovered exoplanets with potential for life, and our satellites are what give us GPS (see page 228), weather mapping and communication networks. But space exploration in recent years has suffered for want of motivation. At the height of the Cold War (in 1966), space exploration accounted for 4.4 per cent of US federal spending. Today, it's 0.44 per cent. What space travel needs is *incentive*. If only Armstrong had come back saying there was oil or mountains of gold on the moon. If that were the case, we'd all be living in moon colonies by now.

GPS

They Know Where You Are

I'm a huge fan of the 'You Are Here' arrow. The bigger and brighter the better. In the labyrinthine money-sink that is a shopping centre, I like to know where I am. In a dizzyingly designed theme park, it's nice to be able to find the nearest ice cream. Thanks to GPS and the internet age, we now have a near-constant access to our very own, personalised 'You Are Here' arrow.

Throw yourself back to an age before GPS, when great swathes of time were wasted squinting at road names or local landmarks just to find out where you were. That's infuriating enough if you're a lost tourist, but when you're in a combat situation, that wasted time might mean death. Which is why GPS, like so many inventions, began in the military.

Invented in the first decades of the 1900s, and finessed during the Second World War, 'radionavigation systems' transformed navigation. These systems usually involved transmitting different Morse code signals in various directions, and using the overlapping of these transmissions to triangulate your location. Up until the 1970s, techniques like this were how the military located things. But in the US Department of Defence, something more ambitious was being cooked up.

GPS involves having satellites orbiting the Earth, which fire their own signals down to us on the ground. GPS satellites have an incredibly precise time stamp on their transmitted signals, so receivers on the ground can tell exactly how long the signal took to get from space. How quickly it arrives tells you your exact distance from the satellite. As long as there are at least four GPS satellites doing this, you can work out exactly where any receiver is on the planet.

When GPS was first invented, its use was highly protected and limited – not only because it gave a powerful military advantage but because receivers were hugely expensive. What few people saw coming, though, was just how quickly the size and price of these receivers would drop. They became so cheap that by the time of the Gulf War in 1990, 90 per cent of all 'military' GPS systems were bought from the commercial sector. Today, we do not need dedicated receivers; chances are you have one built into the phone in your pocket right now.

GPS is now so commonplace that we perhaps forget the geopolitical angle. It's a system paid for and run by Americans. Since it went globally operational in 1995, the US has never weaponised access to it. But it could. This is why the EU with its Galileo system, Russia with its GLONASS and China with its BeiDou system have made sure to wean themselves off USA dependency.

Today, GPS has changed how we go about our daily lives. We are rarely, if ever, entirely lost. Even if we're in a field in the middle of nowhere.

The Internet
Can't Live Without It

You've made an awful mistake: you've told your father-in-law you're driving somewhere new. He takes a breath – this'll be a long one.

'Right, you'll want to take the ring road for twenty miles, then take Exit 43, eastbound, for roughly fifty miles. Then, at the Happy Diner café, turn off ...' You stop listening. You're just going to use Google Maps, as you always do.

This is just one of the many ways that the internet has utterly transformed our lives. Never before in human history has so much information, and so much help, been couched in your pocket.

To understand the internet, we have to go back to those happy days of imminent human extinction – the Cold War. In a world where two disturbingly belligerent superpowers were parading their nuclear arsenals, it became obvious that whoever struck first would have the upper hand. If one nuclear weapon could knock out the communications network of an entire country, then there was no Mutually Assured Destruction (see page 156) at all – one strike and your opponent would be out of the game. What was needed was a *network* of computers without such a centralised weakness. A system that could operate and continue even if one of its terminals was thermonuclearly incinerated. And so ARPANET came into being in the 1970s.

The army did their army things, academics did their academic things and nerds did their nerdy things, all working on ARPANET ... for twenty years. In that time, they developed email, the modem, discussion boards, emoticons, domains and so on. In 1994, certain private companies (called internet service providers) were allowed in on the fun, and so what had been a niche reserve of programmers and computer scientists became much more commonplace.

The internet today is what's called a 'general-purpose technology' – which means that modern society couldn't function without it. Imagine a world without Google or Wikipedia, Facebook or WhatsApp – a reversion back to telephones and letters, encyclopaedias and paper maps. But the reason the internet is a GPT today is the behind-the-scenes stuff; banks, governments, armies and the Illuminati all depend on it.

But things are not all rosy. Whereas before, all knowledge had to pass certain gatekeepers – be they book editors, academics or trained experts – today, anyone with the internet can say what they want. We still don't know what lasting damage has been done to how we think and how we learn.

What's certain, though, is that the internet has changed who we are and how we live more than probably any other technology. For millennia, it was unlikely that you knew what was happening in the next valley over. Now, we can watch pandas in Shanghai, order furniture from Mombasa and videocall a friend in Puerto Rico, all without leaving the sofa.

Social Media

Keep On Scrolling

If I were to look at your most-used apps or websites, I could make a pretty accurate guess as to your age. Are you big into TikTok? You're probably between sixteen and twenty-five years old. Instagram? Definitely under forty. Only use Facebook? Well, you've probably got kids and remember Thatcher's third term.

Almost everyone reading this will use some form of social media – be it YouTube, Snapchat or WhatsApp. It's the surest sign that we're irrevocably wired into the machine. If anyone, in a fit of quixotic technophobia, tries to abandon their smartphone, it's social media that most often calls them back, luring them helplessly towards the twin rocks of procrastination and digital addiction.

It was not always so. The first social media websites – places like Friendster (2002) and MySpace (2003) – were limited by the fact that you needed a computer to access them. What's more, even when the genre-defining Facebook came out, it was a bit like shouting in an empty room. But not for long. Facebook began as a Harvard-only network, then widened to universities generally before going public in 2006. Its rise was astronomical – from zero to 2.3 billion users in fifteen years. It works because everyone and their dog (*literally* their dog) is on Facebook. It's a photo depository, business directory and stalker's paradise in one.

Facebook showed the world (and Silicon Valley investors) that 'social media' was a thing. Within a few years, YouTube (2005), Twitter (2006) and Instagram (2010) all popped up, each dominating their own online niche. But the thing that *really* catalysed social media was the smartphone. When Apple released its iPhone in 2007, with apps and everywhere-you-go internet, it turned social media from being an 'hour or so before bed' thing into 'I can't even go to the toilet without checking my feed'. Today, twice as many users access social media on their phones than on desktop, and many newer social media companies no longer bother with web versions at all.

Social media has transformed society. We are never more than a pocket's glance away from our friends and family, and we can follow the lives of people we've not seen for years. It connects disparate, lonely people while empowering voices like #MeToo and Black Lives Matter. It's made the world a far more open, transparent and connected place.

But, as with a lot of technologies in this book, what began as something relatively well-intentioned has morphed into something insidious. Social media works on algorithms, data mining and monetising user-generated content. It's built to grab your attention and sell your information. It's only recently that society has woken up to the fact that an always-on-display world might be deeply damaging to our souls. In many ways, social media has perverted what 'social' used to mean.

That said, I'm off to check my Insta (@philosophyminis) – go on, give me a follow!

Artificial Intelligence
The Age of Tomorrow

The American computer scientist Marvin Minsky defined artificial intelligence as 'the science of making machines do things that would require intelligence if done by men'. Which sounds hard, but when you think about it, it's actually quite a low bar. Humans do a *lot* of lowbrow 'intelligent' things. We can tell the time; we can add two and two; we can make sounds. All require intelligence, and all can easily be done by machines. So, if we're going by Minsky's definition, then we've had AI for a long time already.

But most of us don't understand AI in this way. Most of us want our machines to do higher-order intelligence – recognise faces, hold conversations, plan for the future, even create art. Here, the issue gets a bit more complex. In the 1980s, the philosopher John Searle spent a lot of time thinking about AI, not least because it was a fantastic tool with which to study our own human intelligence. Searle gave us two distinctions, which we still operate within today – a weak and strong artificial intelligence.

A lot of the AI we have is 'weak artificial intelligence', which means that it might be very good at one or a few tasks but can't do anything more than that. We have facial recognition software, chatbots and systems that can create artworks and written content. We also have robots that can navigate a room, avoiding obstacles. But these are all specialist AIs that are usually very expensive and often error-prone.

While most people reading this will have a small smart device in their pockets that can do a great many AI tasks, none of us carries a workable 'strong' or general intelligence. According to Searle, a machine can be said to have strong artificial intelligence if it has a variety of cognitive functions. This means it can be great (or at least competent) across a whole manner of tasks. A twelve-year-old in a single school day will do maths, art, French and creative writing. At break, they'll talk to friends and read others' emotions. At lunch, they'll run, catch or jump. And, at the end of the day, they'll filter their experiences and retain what's useful. There's no existing AI that can do all of that.

... But we're getting closer. The futurologist Ray Kurzweil argues that with the rate of exponential growth we're seeing in technology, that terrifyingly powerful AI is not very far away. For example, if we were to double the processing power of a computer every year, within seven of these 'doublings', our computers' power would have increased 128-fold.

Technology has a habit of getting away from us. When Gary Kasparov beat a chess computer in 1992, he scoffed at how rubbish it was. Five years later, it beat him. Perhaps we're at a similar point with AI. We might ridicule Siri and Alexa, but in ten years' time, they might be your boss.

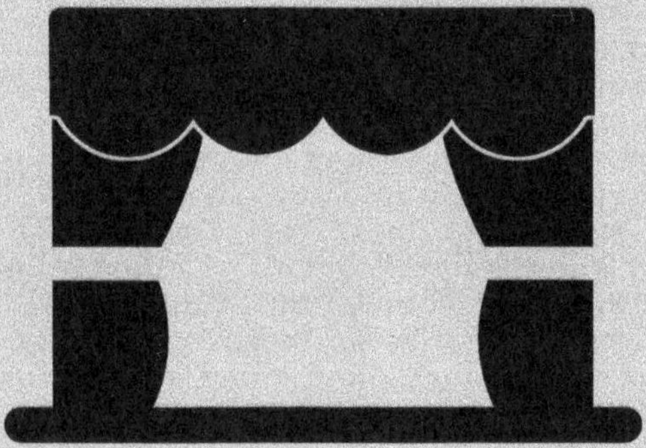

Culture

The year is 2054, and the governments of the world have finally realised something: culture is pointless. There's no use for it. Art galleries take up valuable real estate, playing an instrument adds nothing to GDP and reading books is self-indulgent frippery. In 2054, schools teach only STEM subjects. Society is utilitarian to its core. And yet people have never been less happy. The world is bland, joyless and cold.

Culture is all those acts of human creativity that make life glow – it's what teaches us empathy, shows us beauty and makes our spirit soar.

Poetry

Rhyming, Reciting and Regaling

There's a language called 'parentese'. You'll probably know it. Parentese is the slow, exaggerated, vowel-stressed language of someone talking to a young child. Its use is likely evolutionary. Because parentese is the best way to teach a child your language – it highlights the important bits, and it goes to the right parts of their brain. One way to speak good parentese is to use rhymes. When we use the beat and pattern of simple rhymes, we not only expand our child's vocabulary but they're much, much easier for a child to remember.

Songs, poems and lyrical works are some of the first artforms we know about, probably because of how easily we can retain and retell them. When Genghis Khan (1162–1227) was busy conquering most of Eurasia, he needed messengers to carry his instructions across hundreds of miles, over many weeks. So, every soldier was instructed to learn two or three standard melodies. If they were selected to be a messenger, they turned the message into lyrics and hinged them to these long-remembered songs. A great aide-mémoire to aid massacre.

The Epic of Gilgamesh and the *Iliad* tell us that poetry goes back a very long way. It was likely recited in taverns, on the road, at court and at sea, over and over again. In the same way you probably hum to yourself as you're washing up, the ancients would be retelling legends and stories using those poems.

Early poetry was not only entertaining but also a keystone of national and cultural identity. In addition, it gives us a fascinating insight into the evolution of language. In *Beowulf*, *The Song of Roland* or *The Tale of Genji*, we see how far the words we speak have changed.

The other reason that poetry is such an important element of the human condition is that it speaks to a part of ourselves that normal, literal language cannot. Shakespeare writes, 'My grief lies all within; / And these external manners of laments / Are merely shadows to the unseen grief / That swells with silence in the tortured soul.' He uses words to describe the indescribable. It's language that lets you feel *seen* when public-facing words just won't do. In metaphor, allegory and poetry, we can *feel* what lies behind the words.

Today, poetry has been replaced by song. Poetry tends to sell poorly, and the bestselling poets are usually long dead. But the music industry earns $15 billion a year. In Bob Dylan, Joni Mitchell, Leonard Cohen, Patti Smith or Kendrick Lamar we find the inheritors of poetry. In 2011, Jay Z said about rap, 'If you take those lyrics and you pull them away from the music ... people would say, "This is genius!"'

Poetry is a part of our being, so poetry is not dead – it cannot die, so long as we are here. It's just that today it has a backing track.

Dance

The Moving of Your Soul

There is nothing that expresses naked human emotion more than dancing. There's something pure and good about imagining a person, on their own, without pretence or worry, moving to music. From the silly, frantic, ridiculous bouncing around of two young friends on a sugar high to the sombre funereal sway of mourners, dancing is one of the oldest expressions of human culture. We find passion in the sweaty fug of a Brazilian samba club. We find worship in the rhythmic whirling of Sufi mystics. We find love in the slow, close embrace of an elderly couple at their granddaughter's wedding.

The way that a person dances can tell you a lot about them. It tells you about their personality, their body and their culture. If you think about the world of difference between a ballerina's pirouette, a breakdancer's spin, a Scot's ceilidh march or a Native American's jumping pow wow, what you're seeing is different attitudes to life. How we move our bodies, and how we show that movement to the world (or even to our gods), is structural to being human. Dance can be a ritual – with costumes, sacred spaces and a desired intention (good fortune, divine blessing, romantic display, etc.).

It is also hugely social. For example, in Greek culture, dancing exists to create what's called *kefi*. *Kefi* is a kind of togetherness and communal energy that breaks down animosity and lifts everyone up. It's seen as an essential element in a celebration. Across much of Central and Southern Africa, if a community is described as 'sick', they might be prescribed *ngoma*. *Ngoma* can be the name for a certain kind of drum, the act of drumming or the dancing and emotions their playing evokes. When a group of people are at loggerheads, they are told to listen to and dance along with *ngoma*. The idea is that those who dance together, stay together.

But if we treat dance too closely as a social, historical phenomenon, we miss one obvious fact: dancing is really good for you. First, it is a form of exercise, which keeps the body healthy and improves our coordination. But there's also a lot of research to show that it makes us happy – multiple studies prove that dancing releases dopamine (the happy hormone) and can even alleviate certain mental-health conditions.

Dancing is enjoying a revival today. Partly it's because of certain popular television shows, and partly it's because thirty minutes of Zumba is a great way to keep you fit. A lot of it, too, has to do with a modern rejection of the historic prudish and puritanical disregard for dance. We are much more aware, these days, of the need to express ourselves, let ourselves go, be part of a group or just be silly for a bit. What better way to do all of this than by dancing?

Writing

Just Squiggles on a Page

Can you imagine not being able to read? Look at these words now and try to see them as the same nonsense squiggles an illiterate child would see. Ultimately, that's all they are: lines and dots in a particular order and shape that we decode into concepts. And these squiggles transformed the world. Once writing came along, humans learned how to disseminate and pass on all their gathered knowledge. With writing, we could stand on the shoulders of giants.

We know that writing first emerged in Mesopotamia around 3400 BCE. *Homo sapiens* had been around for nearly 200,000 years before this, and it's no accident that writing first emerged when humans became sedentary, threw up walls and started to form a complex society. This is because writing was first and foremost the trader's skill, used for keeping track of accounts. It was an aide-mémoire for all your orders, contracts, outgoings, debts and so on. In fact, it was likely that the earliest societies, far from seeing writing as a sign of status and culture, looked down on it as a peasant's tool.

But once the seed of writing was planted, a huge literary tree bloomed. The first systems, known as 'pictographic', were essentially little doodles of the things they represented – a drawing of a sheaf of wheat would represent wheat, for example. The earliest Egyptian hieroglyphs were of this kind. But then, quite abruptly (in ancient history terms), humans developed the 'rebus principle', where the pictographic symbols represented both the word and the *sound*. So, a bird would be both a bird and the syllabic sound (phoneme) 'bird'. Stringing these phonemes together would allow more complicated words and, of course, a much more symbolic and rich writing system. Thanks to the rebus principle, we could now write about abstract and intangible things, like justice or magic.

Some societies, like the Chinese and Japanese today, keep a variation on this pictographic rebus principle (Japanese has a symbol for each syllable). Others, though, developed alphabets.

The problem with symbols for everything is, as you find in Chinese Hanzi characters, that you need thousands and thousands of them. The wonder of the alphabet is its efficiency. With only a fraction of the graphemes (squiggles), you can represent pretty much all the sounds in your culture's language. It's thought that the optimum alphabet in terms of accuracy:efficiency is twenty to thirty characters. Many dead scripts fell away precisely because they were either too accurate (and so laborious to learn) or too efficient (and so had too many ambiguities).

Writing changed the world. Thanks to ancient Middle Eastern masons and fishmongers, we can now access the minds of people all around the world, and across five millennia. Writing educates and informs, and transports us to wonderful and fantastic lands of our imagination.

The Printing Press
A Chancer Who Changed the World

You've been hunched over the manuscript for five hours straight. The candle is flickering, and your eyes are exhausted. You have long lost sensation in your writing hand. Five hours on the dullest, most tedious pages of the Book of Numbers, and for what? The glory of God, you guess.

This was largely how books were made for most of history – by hard graft and careful work. We even have evidence of monks writing cheeky commentaries on their manuscripts, like 'Oh, my hand', 'The parchment is hairy' and even 'For Christ's sake, give me a drink'. So, we know at least a few scribes welcomed the arrival of the printing press.

Johannes Gutenberg (c. 1393–1406) was a chancer. He started out selling 'magic mirrors' to pilgrims so they could 'store' the healing powers of relics. But when plague came to town and put him out of business, he headed downriver to Strasbourg to try something else. And thank the holy relics he did.

Like Guglielmo Marconi (see page 222), Gutenberg was not so much an inventor as a *compiler* of existing technology. There were three major aspects to his printing press, and they all existed many years before Gutenberg.

First, there was 'moveable' type – carved letters that could be rearranged to make words – which had been used for centuries in China and the Middle East. Second, there was the artisan metallurgy of European blacksmiths and miners. And finally, there were the wine or olive presses that had existed since antiquity.

Gutenberg's genius lay in how he brought all these together. He used foundries to mass produce hundreds of letters, which had previously had to be painstakingly carved by hand (the word 'font' derives from the Latin for foundry), and he used a modified press to produce uniform and quick inking of pages.

It's hard to overstate the impact of the printing press. Gutenberg's version actually produced only about 150 books, all of which were Bibles, but once the idea was out there, there was no stopping it. In the 1450s, there were a few hundred printed books; by the 1500s there were millions. Ironically, given Gutenberg saw his press as a way to standardise the Roman Catholic Bible, it popularised Martin Luther's *Ninety-five Theses* and the Reformation (Luther didn't know his Theses had been taken away and printed – the first example of unwittingly going viral).

The mass production of books allowed ideas to spread like never before. It ushered in the first information age. Scholars could now acquaint themselves with the ancient wisdom of Plutarch or Aristotle. Theologians could get their hands on actual Bibles and not have to rely on priests as gatekeepers. Scientists could read, check and develop each other's work. It's not an exaggeration to say Gutenberg shepherded in the Renaissance, the Reformation and the Scientific Revolution. Not bad for someone who once lived off scamming pilgrims.

Education

This Is What You Should Know

Imagine you're the first person, ever, to set up a school. What would it look like? What would be on the curriculum? Would just anyone be allowed in? What kind of teachers would there be?

The idea that we should actively teach things to young people is a relatively new one. And the notion this should be accessible to all people, regardless of wealth, gender or status, was positively unthinkable for much of history. It still is in some parts of the world.

Before the school, there were more informal education networks, and these are *ancient*. If we include a father teaching his daughter how to throw a spear, then it would even be prehistoric. But the notion of a formal, curriculum-type system only comes about with the advent of large cities and complex bureaucracies (see page 170).

In China, the imperial examination for civil servants began in around the seventh century, and tutors and schools sprang up to help candidates pass it. In royal courts across Europe, clerks, pages and attendants were educated for the sole purpose of statecraft. Writing itself (see page 242) first began as a bureaucrat's tool – it was initially considered common and unworthy of aristocrats.

In fact, the first medieval universities, from the earliest in Bologna to the big names like Oxford or Sorbonne, initially began as schools for would-be lawyers, theologians and physicians. As civil law and ecclesiastical bureaucracy became more convoluted, it became clear that a uniform, rigorous education was required. If doctors in Padua were learning a different physiology from those in Milan, something needed to be fixed. The very word 'universitas' implied some kind of universal standard, and having a degree became a sign that you were one of the gang.

Of course, education is not just about acquiring technical skills. In fact, Plato and Aristotle argued that this is the very opposite of what it should be. They saw education as a means to discover what was true about the world. Plato believed that maths, astronomy and music (to a degree) were the highest educational tools available to us.

And this sense of pupils being 'seekers of truth' is education's greatest asset. In the earliest universities, students had to participate in a 'disputation', which finds its modern equivalent in the dissertation process. To our eyes, this would look like a debating chamber – the idea being that to be a good student you must challenge, criticise and analyse everything.

To become educated, in other words, means to question things. Of course, in the past this had its rules (certain political or religious topics were off-limits) but from the Middle Ages onwards, the educated were also the revolutionaries and innovators of society. Learning this or that is useful, but far more important is the critical-thinking skills it gives you. The more you learn, the less you simply accept, and humanity progresses because of it.

History

It's Murky Back There

Imagine if all you knew of the past was what your grandparents could tell you. There you all are, gathered around the fireplace, children huddled together, all kept rapt by the wizened old codger telling tales of the 'old times'. With wafting arms and a dramatic voice, he'll rattle on about this war, that legend, those people. Stories of past sporting victories and leaders are all passed down via these slightly hammy monologues. No doubt this is entertaining, but is it what you would call *history*?

There's a part of human nature that wants to understand the past. It gives us clues to who we are today and advice on where we should go. So, making sure that we get an accurate, recorded account of what *actually* happened matters.

The *Epic of Gilgamesh*, from the second millennium BCE, is the oldest substantial piece of literature we have. It offers historians a window into the social and political order of the first civilisations. But it also involves a pub in the underworld, roaming ghosts and magic flowers. Later, Herodotus, often called the 'father of [Western] history', is an invaluable source regarding the Greco-Persian Wars. Yet his accounts of a king's mistress giving birth to a lion and of gold-digging ants foraging for their owners do seem a touch unlikely.

The first *reliable* history – one which sought to be true to fact – came from China. The *Twenty-four Histories* were authoritative accounts of various empires compiled mainly from court records and primary sources. In the Western world, although Herodotus gets all the glory, his contemporary Thucydides was much better at gathering actual historical evidence. Where Herodotus saw history as scripted by the gods, Thucydides saw it as a human, worldly thing, driven by cause and effect. There was *historical method* to what he did, which essentially amounts to three operations:

First, it involves research – a good historian cannot settle for one source or one angle.

Second, it's critical of the sources. It must rationalise the implausible, take account for biases, cross-reference and so on.

Third, it weighs up the sources and the criticisms, and develops the most plausible narrative.

The problem is that the past is a murky place. When you 'do history', it's like doing a jigsaw where a fair few of the pieces are missing and you've no real idea what it's meant to look like.

The historian's job is similar to that of a judge. There's a story to be found, a truth to be drawn out, but it requires attention and evaluation. It means saying, 'Hang on, this wizard and Round Table stuff sounds a bit far-fetched' (Geoffrey of Monmouth) or 'I'm not sure there's much evidence for Cyclopes and griffins living in Europe' (Herodotus again). Historians look for the truth about where we come from, even when it might be a *bit* less magical than those old codger's tales.

Western Classical Music
Polyphonic Pleasantries

If you were born in the second half of the eighteenth century, and you ate your vegetables and lived a healthy life, you could have heard Mozart, Beethoven, Schubert, Chopin, Mendelssohn and Wagner originals. You could have been in the front row for the first performance of the *Symphony No. 9* or *The Marriage of Figaro*. The thing about classical music is that we often think of it as timeless. All those famous pieces you hear in adverts or at state events seem to have always existed – they are the background noise that we in the West unthinkingly inherit.

But classical music was, once, the pop music to a generation. Wagner had his superfans (Hitler, not least) and people would rush to hear the new Brahms banger. These huge, groundbreaking names of musical history were just people, tapping out tunes on a piano at 3 a.m. Each of them was as genre-defining and genre-*breaking* in their own time as The Beatles, Black Sabbath or Tupac Shakur have been in ours.

It's likely there's been music for as long as humans have had a voice, but we can only know anything about that music when people (usually monks) started to write it down. For a long time, music was monophonic – which meant it had a single melody with no accompaniment. Gregorian chants follow one tune, in chorus or alone, and they're no less beautiful for it.

From the ninth century, musicians dabbled with chords, still mostly in choirs, until the Renaissance Period (1400–1600) popularised 'polyphonic' melodies. Having multiple harmonies makes for a much richer listening experience. It seems to be universally true that all humans *know* what is dissonant or consonant – such as the 'perfect fifth' ending to a melody – but whether we call dissonance unpleasant or not depends on our time and culture. Dissonant clashes are common in East Asian or Arabic classical music.

The Baroque Period (1600–1750) gave us a sophisticated tonal system, with more interesting use of major and minor keys, which in turn developed a move to orchestral pieces. It became apparent that certain instruments were better suited to create different effects. This all culminated in the great symphony movements of the Classical Period (1750–1820), which was all about form and elegance, and then the Romantic Period (1830–1910), which focused on expression and emotion.

You don't have to know anything about classical music to *feel* it. When you listen to the right piece at the right time, you can feel your soul lurch. There's something mournful about a cello concerto and something rousing about a national anthem. There's a frisson when you hear the *Star Wars* theme tune and *Ride of the Valkyries* is so exciting that researchers named it as the most dangerous music to listen to while driving. As billions of humans for many centuries can attest, there's something profoundly rapturous about the sound of an orchestra in full flow.

The Novel

A Woman's Form

We are a storytelling species. From prehistoric caves to IMAX cinemas, from the *Ramayana* to *Star Wars*, we love a good yarn. Yet the *way* we tell stories has changed considerably in the last 300 years. Medieval scholars reading modern novels would be as surprised by the style as much as by the content. Most of the stories (we know of) up until the eighteenth century were about events, with very few fleshed-out, complicated *characters*. For instance, the *Iliad* features hardly any commentary on the heroes' psychology and the Old Testament has little in terms of inner monologue. They're simply narrative accounts of things happening.

This all changes with the novel.

It's hard to pin down exactly what makes a novel different from what came before but we can see three elements that come up again and again. First, a novel must have *characters* at its centre – a protagonist we learn about, usually in great depth. Second, it must be written in prose rather than verse. Third, it must be, at least partially, fictional. Of course, these are not 'rules', *per se*. As always, there are post-modern, avant-garde and experimental types tearing up conventions. But, for now, they will have to do.

It used to be thought that *Don Quixote* was the first modern novel but recently (and less Europe-centrically) we've come to identify far older examples of the form. The *Theologus Autodidactus* by Arab physician Ibn al-Nafis in the thirteenth century, for example, has a good claim. Older still is an eleventh-century Japanese work called *The Tale of Genji* by Lady Murasaki Shikibu. It's the story of Genji, the artistic, gentle, illegitimate son of the emperor and his journey through court life.

It's telling that the oldest known novel was written by a woman. The literary scholar Ruth Perry described the novel as 'a woman's form, as the sentimental inheritors of the epics of men'. Her point is that novels are about everyday life. They are not about wars, monster slaying or big historical events. The novel is about what happens inside a mind over a single life – often a female one.

Alongside the first 'great novels', like *Robinson Crusoe*, there were the 'amatory novels'. These romantic novellas, as we'd call them, are often overlooked today, and the names Eliza Haywood, Aphra Behn and Delarivier Manley are smudged from cultural history. Jane Austen, however, cannot so easily be erased. Her satirical, light and comedic tone coupled with OG period drama showed just how exciting, insightful and innovative the novel can be.

Women novelists, and women readers, are what helped propel novels to where they sit today – dominating the book market. The top twenty bestselling books of all time are all novels. *Don Quixote*, by Cervantes, has sold ten times the number of the bestselling non-religious non-fiction book (*You Can Heal Your Life* by Louise Hay). It's fair to say that novels have changed our reading habits forever.

Perspective
Painting into the Distance

Let's be honest, most paintings before the Renaissance were pretty rubbish. Historically invaluable and often decoratively beautiful, no doubt, but just have a look at them. They're almost always flat, with warped proportions and blank-faced figures. Apart from a few exceptions, artists for a thousand years had no sense of perspective and dimension.

Which is why the introduction of the idea of a 'central vanishing point', or perspective, was so revolutionary.

It's highly unlikely that early medieval artists didn't know *how* to draw perspective, but rather it was consciously rejected. Perspective is important if you intend to represent something realistically. But if you intend to evoke some emotional or religious idea through your work, then other techniques might be more important.

In fact, representationalism was once seen as positively egregious. Plato believed that representational art was nothing more than trickery which could weaken the intellect and tie us too closely to this world. And, given that almost all Western art after the Romans was Christian art, it's likely God-fearing artists followed suit. After all, art ought to encourage devotion, the contemplation of the Lord. What's the point of perspective if it simply reproduces what we can see with our eyes?

This changed with the fairly unknown architect Filippo Brunelleschi. Around 1415, Brunelleschi gave a public demonstration of perspective. For a thousand years, people had come to believe that realism was to be shunned. In the fifteenth century, though, humanism was on the table. People wanted to see lifelike portrayals of the world. So painters started experimenting with the idea of a central vanishing point. Within fifty years, everyone from graffiti artists to the most renowned painters of the day were adding perspective to their work. It was like there had never been any other way.

There were huge religious and intellectual implications to this. Suddenly, the material and everyday things around us had a value of their own, and with the increasingly realistic depictions of *humans*, a subtle secularism and individualism worked its way into art.

But perspective changed other things too. Designs or schematics for new inventions could now be made, reproduced and sent all over the world. For instance, an Italian astronomer (Galileo: see page 65) could read and recreate the designs of a telescope first presented in the Netherlands. What's more, engineering and geometry developed their own versions of the central vanishing point in 'orthographic projection'. Not only did this unlock much more intricate architectural designs, but it made map-making more accurate for a spherical globe.

It seems odd to think of 3D drawing as a big idea, but it really was a leap forward. And even though it was known and selectively used in the ancient world, it wasn't until a few Italian artists popularised it that it came to dominate pretty much any profession that required any kind of draughtsmanship.

Theatre
Thespians and Luvvies

We are all actors. We wear costumes to present an image, we say our lines to portray a certain character and we behave socially as our cues tell us – otherwise: *'Exit, pursued by bear.'* As Shakespeare also famously wrote, 'All the world's a stage, / And all the men and women merely players.' There's a dance and ritual to almost all of what we do. And so, in many ways, the history of theatre is the history of simply being human. When my toddler picks up a stick and gives a Blackbeard-worthy 'Arrr!', he's acting. When my aunt pretends to be Elvis over a boardgame at Christmas, that's a stage.

It's no surprise, then, that the theatre – or some kind of spectacle – goes as far back as records allow. For the most part, this was simply the recitation or acting out of a story – usually a religious one. While Greece is often viewed as the birthplace of theatre, we also see in ancient Egypt, for instance, plays about Isis, Horus and Seth, replete with stage directions and hippopotamus props. But in Athens, we have the advent of 'drama' as an art form. We have stories *designed* for the stage, with lines, stagecraft and theatrical spectacle. During the annual Festival of Dionysius there was often a drama competition, and Euripides and Aristophanes cut their teeth there.

In Roman society, actors were *infames* – notorious layabouts who occupied the lowest rung of society. How could we trust professional liars, after all? So, when the Emperor Nero (notorious for his brutal streak) insisted on acting and singing for his dinner guests, it was likely somewhat awkward. In modern terms, it would be like an unhinged, murderous warlord Morris-dancing naked and asking you to applaud him.

Theatre has been enjoyed across the world for millennia. It meant escapism, laughter, high emotion and raucous cheering. Which, if you were a Puritan in the seventeenth century, sounded like the devil's work. William Prynne, a leading Puritan voice of the time, saw the theatre as a seething, diabolical barrel of 'wanton gestures; amorous kisses, complements, and salutes; meretricious songs and speeches; lascivious whorish Actions; beautiful faces; ravishing music, flexanimous enticements, witty obscenities, rhetorical passages [and] adulterous representations'. Today, that sounds like a pretty good advert for going to the theatre.

Of course, we cannot discuss the theatre without mentioning William Shakespeare. Shakespeare turned (European) theatre from a slightly hammy and drunken affair into high culture. He invented around 1,700 words and he's still quoted today, in the streets and in government. It's not an exaggeration to say that almost all modern movies can be mapped onto a Shakespeare play. In his works, we see the near-perfection of almost all methods of storytelling.

Humans are actors and we all enjoy a spectacle (even if we secretly prefer our toddler's pirate to Shakespeare's *Othello*).

Fashion
Still Wearing Flares

What are you wearing right now? This isn't a sleazy Tinder message but an exercise in sartorial reflection. More accurately, *why* are you wearing those clothes? Some people will be wearing their old, comfortable pyjamas or slacks. Others will be strapped into impractical, rigid garments but looking dandy and dapper as heck. Most of us will be somewhere in between. But whether you're wearing a frayed dressing gown or a cocktail dress, you'll have done so thanks to fashion. Fashion is one of the most underappreciated big ideas in this book. Unless you're 'in the business', you'll likely not have thought much about why you wear those trousers or do your hair that way.

It's all to do with elegance, taste and being *à la mode*.

Fashion is, quite broadly, what society considers beautiful or stylish, but it's also an expression *of* that society. So, a tribal face paint or a clan's characteristic jewellery would be fashion. Anything beyond the merely practical – any colour, cut, stitching or frill – is fashion. But fashion also comes attached with value judgements. You want to wear a certain outfit so people get the right impression of what you do and who you are – it tells us about your wealth, your job, your status, your country, your time and your values. Compare a geisha to a goth or a City banker to a jihadist – why have they chosen that outfit? Everything we wear is a statement.

Up until the fourteenth century, almost everyone in Europe dressed the same. There was no such thing as men's and women's fashion – it was loose drapes and practical cuts for everyone. Then, around 1350, with the introduction of fasteners like button and toggles, things changed. Suddenly clothes could *fit*. They hugged the body, and you could actually tell if the person under all those rags were male or female. As with any new fashion (even today), people were scandalised. To see the curvature of a woman or the musculature of a man ... it was enough to make God blush! Nevertheless, from then on, the rate of change in fashion increased exponentially.

Fashion is not only a way of flaunting yourself but can also be a protest (and its corollary: oppression). 'Sumptuary laws' made the act of wearing certain clothes illegal for certain people – for instance, an Englishman wearing a kilt during the Scottish uprisings or when King Louis XIII banned commoners from wearing lace or metallic embroidery. Modern North Korea has banned anyone but their Supreme Leader from wearing a leather coat.

It's easy to laugh at yesterday's fashion – the oversized ruffs and ridiculous wigs – but today's fashion will soon become tomorrow's laughing stock. Take a photo of yourself at a party and come back to it in forty years' time. After you stop cringing, you'll be able to appreciate how much has changed. It's how fashion has always operated.

Professional Sport

Your Team Are Rubbish

By most definitions, professional sport is simply sport that earns someone money. If we're being strictly accurate (which would exclude the time I was awarded £5 for hula hooping at a kid's party), it might be a sport that's your *only* source of income. Professional sport also involves organisation, fans, league tables and international fixtures.

Professional sports go back a very long way indeed. The first example we know about is ancient Egyptian, 5,000 years ago. Under the watchful (and paying) eye of the pharaoh, there would have been a great number of sporting events to honour the gods at religious festivals. We've found mural pictures of archery, handball, hockey, javelin, swimming and gymnastics, for example.

But it was the Olympic Games – those tests of prowess devoted to the god Zeus – that have come to define 'organised sports'. The Games go back to around the eighth century BCE, and originally featured chariot racing and a brutal, naked wrestling match called the *pankration* – the only rules being no gouging, biting or attacks on genitals. The Olympic Games were (and are) the ultimate test in ability across a huge range of disciplines, and this is a good opportunity to lament those events now lost to mean-spirited Olympic committees, including the tug of war, croquet and hot-air ballooning.

Even in the ancient world, being good at sport could make you a ton. The Roman chariot games really were the football of the ancient world – with packed *stadia* (a Latin word for the length of a racecourse), overpriced merchandise and hooliganism. The charioteer Gaius Appuleius Diocles is thought to have earned the equivalent of $15 billion in today's money – making him possibly the richest sportsperson in history.

Huge spectator events and professional sports took a millennia-long hiatus during the medieval period (partly because there were fewer densely packed cities). These were replaced by local pub games like chess or axe-throwing for the commoners, or jousting or mock fights called 'melees' for the nobles.

Today, professional sport is one of the most important pastimes for the vast majority of the world's population. Most people spend at least a bit of time watching others play sport every week, whether it's cricket, football, sprinting or table tennis. In his book *Homo Ludens*, Johan Huizinga argues that all human activity, viewed a certain way, is a kind of sport. If Huizinga is right, sport is as old as society, and professional sport is inclusive and broad in scope. Which is all to rationalise the 'professional hula hooper' entry on my LinkedIn profile.

Moving Pictures
Crying into Popcorn

Once a thing has become a huge, billion-dollar success, it's hard to imagine a time when it was just a gimmick. I remember owning, when I was younger, one of those blacked-out boxes you put over your eyes into which you could place a slideshow reel of the world's attractions. It was a VR headset but for static photos. Today, VR is the future. What was once a gimmick is now the future of technology.

The same is true for moving pictures. When the first animation devices appeared at the start of the nineteenth century (essentially, fast-moving slide shows), they were treated as novelties. By the end of that century, the Lumière brothers were screening the first motion picture – a popcorn-crunching romp called *Workers Leaving the Lumière Factory*. Today, the film industry is worth about $140 billion and the average American will spend three hours of their waking day watching TV. It's fair to say that moving pictures are no longer a gimmick.

If you want to ruin the nostalgia of a favourite childhood movie, go back and watch it on a modern ultra-HD TV. You'll soon see just how rubbish cinema was, not that long ago. The quality is grainy, the sets are like cheap school productions, and your last Halloween outfit probably had better prosthetics. Movies have a way of getting better without you realising – but very occasionally you get to witness one of those 'this changes everything' moments.

In 1921, for instance, when Charlie Chaplin's *The Kid* was released, it showed just how emotionally resonant a motion-picture narrative could be – at times hilarious, at others deeply moving. When Disney released *Snow White and the Seven Dwarves* in 1937, it proved an animated children's tale could work as a full-length feature. When *2001: A Space Odyssey* (1968) and *Star Wars* (1977) came out, they showed the power of good cinematography – if you could imagine it, a director could show it. And, when the Marvel Cinematic Universe got going, it gave a whole new meaning to the words 'big-budget epic'.

Today, film is not limited to Holly-, Bolly- or Nollywood. Most smartphones these days can take video footage in 4K quality using great motion-tracking software. So it's no wonder that the younger generations are turning to TikTok and YouTube instead of their nearest cinema. While the over-25s rank TV and movies as their favourite entertainment pastimes, Gen Z prefer gaming, social media and the internet. A worry for the film business, really.

Yet most people reading this will have their favourite film(s) or, at the least, will enjoy a long discussion over what they might be. Movies are deeply personal – they conjure up childhood Christmases on the sofa with your dad, a first date with the love of your life, or a jaw-dropping moment of genuine awe and wonder. Even if how we digest them changes, it's clear that movies still matter.

Pop Music
Smells Like Teen Spirit

It's one of the indisputable facts of life that pop music can be defined as 'that which older generations don't understand'. As we get older, we tend to find the music of today's youth increasingly incomprehensible, uncouth and just ... *noise*. And, as we do so, we can take our place in a long line of history's curmudgeons.

Pop music is not simply about The Beach Boys, Elvis Presley, Adele or The Spice Girls. It's about a stage of your life. It's about teenagerhood. Pop music is the backing track to school discos, road trips and finding your tribe. When we think back on our pop idols and poster pin-ups, the memories come to us stewed in a rich spice of hormones, nostalgia and adolescent fears.

'Pop' music simply means 'popular' at a certain time, and, as a genre, most scholars assume pop emerged around the 1950s. But, if you were to try to describe it more closely, you'd have a hard time of it. Pop music is like a great montage, made up of rock and roll, hip-hop, punk, dance, disco, R&B and so on. Defining pop music is like trying to grip water. The best we can possibly do is to isolate 'big names' in pop – the names who defined their decade, such as The Beatles, Michael Jackson, Rihanna or Taylor Swift. And yet, if you venture beyond the obvious choices, things quickly get heated. For instance, are Queen, Elvis, Bob Dylan or Kendrick Lamar 'pop'? I'll leave you to shout your answers at the page.

Pop music emerged out of the dark, depressing nadir of two world wars. It was tied to a counterculture movement that promoted freedom, liberation and life-affirming passion. It was the antithesis of the square and stuffy prudery of yesteryear. As a result, the label of 'pop' has now come to be laden with a certain kind of baggage. Pop is the frothy, silly, immature obsession of teenagers. There's a certain type of person who'll sneer at you if BTS are your favourite band. *Real* music connoisseurs don't like pop. *Real* musicians hate the pop industry. Yet the pop industry is so huge that if future aliens were to chart the culture of our post-war period they'd be forgiven for thinking pop music *is* music.

Today, close to 90 per cent of all music we listen to comes through streaming services like iTunes or Spotify. And this is having an interesting impact. Because people love *their* pop music from *their* generation, they also like to relisten to it. It's as easy, now, to buy a 1977 album as a 2023 one. As a result, in the USA, *old* songs now represent 70 per cent of the music market. Pop music today is in danger of becoming stagnant in a constant nostalgic replay.

Postcolonial Criticism
National Trauma

When we use the word traumatic, we don't just mean terrible. The events that *cause* trauma are, certainly, terrible. But, for something to be traumatic, it needs to leave a scar. The trauma survivor is irreversibly changed by their experience: their minds and bodies have been forcibly wrenched into a new position. Trauma is relived, as flashbacks or nightmares, so that it becomes a rewiring of the brain. It's a new way of seeing the world. When you've been through trauma, the world gets painted in black hues.

Colonialism was, for many people, a form of trauma. Both on a personal level (i.e., for those who were enslaved, dehumanised or excluded) and on a political level. It leaves a scar on your national psyche, and it defines the landscape in which the nation now operates. Postcolonial criticism is the modern appreciation of this fact.

Postcolonial criticism is the study of the lasting legacies of empire on a global and personal scale, and it can usually be examined in two main forms: through politics and the arts.

In geopolitical terms, postcolonialism refers to an awareness of the lasting inequalities caused by the often ham-fisted administrative policies of colonial powers, which have left a lasting impact on the political and economic system within those countries to this day. The most visible (on a map) and stark example is in Africa. At the 1884 Berlin Conference, the European powers gathered around to divide 'their' countries into neat, ordered, geometric shapes. Before colonialism, most African borders were fuzzy and porous. The prevalence of nomadic tribes or diasporic ethnic populations meant it was nearly impossible to define this or that country according to Western principles. So when France and Britain drew the borders of modern Nigeria, for instance, they created a country made up of over 250 ethnic groups. Most of the instability in Africa today (as in a lot of post-colonial countries) is down to arbitrary borders and extractive administrative mechanisms.

In artistic terms, postcolonialism is an attempt to understand the effect colonialism has had on language, identity and culture. In Toni Morrison's *Beloved*, for instance, we can see the old, deep scars American slavery left on the African-American population. Zadie Smith, Lynn Nottage, Arundhati Roy, Jhumpa Lahiri, Salman Rushdie, Joseph Conrad and many more all, in some way, explore the damage left behind for everyday people living in post-colonial conditions.

The world is complicated. History is an interconnected jumble of power dynamics – featuring both good people and total bastards. But history is often confused with 'forgotten'. Colonialism is not so much historical as it is the everyday, lived reality of the majority of the world's population. Postcolonial theory is an attempt to understand this legacy and what it means to grow up in an unequal world. As with anything, understanding means empathy. Postcolonial criticism is a step towards dismantling the imperialistic narratives that traumatised so many people and subverting those ideals.

Computer Games

Console Wars

When I was at school, I made a mistake that was to haunt me for years to come: I chose SEGA over Nintendo. While all my friends were hunched over their Game Boys and bouncing Mario around oversized, snapping plants, I was collecting golden rings with Sonic. Don't get me wrong, Sonic and I had a great time, but I didn't know how far I was out of kilter with the 1990s UK gaming *zeitgeist*. Now, every so often, for my sins, I have to sit through three hours of slightly drunk friends reciting all manifestations of Pokémon.

For a lot of people reading this, computer games act as a kind of timestamp of the soul. They're the nostalgic flagpoles of our past. When you think about the first computer games you lost yourself in, you also remember the room, the console, the people and the feeling. For many, remembering computer games is a poignant walk back into childhood.

Today, we live in the age of 'console wars', which means would-be gamers will often choose between PlayStation, Xbox, Nintendo or PC (although a great many will, of course, mix it up). But for the first decade or so of computer gaming, there was only one real contender: the Atari 2600. Before its release in 1977, games were basic, limited and often only available to computer scientists. With the Atari 2600, the general public were finally gifted computer games, starting with the genre-defining *Pong*.

Given it was obvious there was a huge market for computer games, the story since has been one of unbounded imagination and dizzying technological developments. In the 1980s, Nintendo and then SEGA released consoles with insertable game cartridges. Computer-game characters suddenly entered the mainstream – first Donkey Kong and then the entire Mario family. Most people, today, will know Lara Croft, Pikachu, Yoshi, Scorpion or Pac-Man. And these characters *matter*. The plotlines of these games are often so immersive that we emotionally engage with their protagonists more than even characters on TV or in books. Computer games have such a strong brand value it's no wonder more and more are being turned into movies.

Up until the last decade or so, computer gaming was still either a childish thing to do or the niche and somewhat embarrassing hobby of nerds and geeks. Now, you'll see CEOs and politicians playing games on their phones. Mobile gaming is a $70 billion industry. What's more, with the technology now so advanced, and the games requiring such skill, the world of esports is a new, exciting reality.

Computer games have gone mainstream. While a lot of people speculate that they're addictive and/or corrupting (especially the violent ones), there's also a lot to be said for them. Computer games are good for your coordination, they involve high levels of social interaction (especially cooperative games) and they make for great, competitive sport. If you haven't already, maybe it's time to pick up a gaming console ...

The On-demand Revolution
The Parable of the Blockbuster

One of the best things about Christmas when growing up was the festive edition of the *Radio Times*. You'd get to pore over all the must-see recommendations but also check out the scribbled circlings of the rest of the family. The *Radio Times* was a fun read but it was also a blueprint for battle. On Boxing Day, your sister might have her eyes on *Home Alone* but you notice it's clashing with *Match of the Day*. There will be blood.

Anyone under the age of twenty will be utterly confused by what I just wrote. The idea that you'd have to *plan* your TV choices or *negotiate* whose choice to watch would be utterly alien. We live today with the everyday fact that you can watch anything you want whenever you want. And if I can't, well, I know a man who knows a fishy website and can get it for me anyway.

The story of the on-demand revolution can be told through the modern-day parable 'The Blockbuster and the Netflix'. Once upon a time, there was an entertainment behemoth known as Blockbuster. With their rows and rows of VHS boxes in shops in every neighbourhood, they dominated the video rental market. Netflix, though, was the young rival trying to carve out a niche that Blockbuster hadn't reached: *the internet.* Blockbuster thought they knew better. They didn't care for digital and thought streaming was a flash in the pan. In one of those 'Oh, you idiot' moments, Blockbuster turned down an offer to buy Netflix for $50 million in 2000. Within ten years, Blockbuster was declared bankrupt and, today, Netflix generates over $30 billion in revenue with over 220 million subscribers worldwide.

The on-demand revolution has changed how we consume media. Traditional gatekeepers like networks and movie studios no longer have a monopoly – *we* control exactly what and when we watch. The result is that there is a much stronger feedback loop these days. Algorithms tell media companies instantly what people are liking or not, and studios will commission or reject a programme simply on the basis of subscribers' viewing history.

For most people, the likes of Amazon Prime, Netflix and Hulu have made watching TV far, far easier (with fewer Christmas fights). But it's not just TV which has become on-demand. Almost all aspects of our lives now are determined by apps, algorithms and delivery drivers leaving £500 items in the pouring rain. With Amazon, Uber, eBay, Just Eat, Etsy and so on, all the world is just a click away. Blockbuster died out not only because it failed to keep up but because it was a bricks and mortar shop that you had to go to. Now, the world will come to us. Give it a few years and perhaps it won't just be Blockbuster who are yesterday's story. Let's face it, we don't need shops any more; there's always an app instead.

Religion
& Belief

A sociology lecturer I had once jokingly remarked,
'If you go to any society, in any time, you'll find two
things: a place or means to get intoxicated and a place
of worship. And the two are often very close.' Because,
as much as the fact might grate with militant atheists,
religion or spirituality is as close to universal as we can
find. A prehistoric boy, looking up at the stars, will see
windows to the god-plane. A mourning mother, burying
her child, will take solace in the concept of afterlife.
A monk will sit for hours in the stillness of meditation,
contemplating the unity of the universe.

Religion and belief are the ways we try to find
meaning in an often bewildering world.

Creation Myths
In the Beginning

In a time before time, the land was asleep. The world was an endless night, everything blanketed in darkness. Then, carried by the winds of eternity, a beautiful song was heard. It sang of light and life, and its melody brought the first dawn. In the liminal grey of the first day, the Ancestors appeared. These were beings of great power and wisdom, and they gave their voices to the song.

With every step the Ancestors took, the world itself took a breath. Trees unfurled their blossoms and mighty rivers surged from the ground. As the celestial song grew louder, more beings joined its chorus. Countless spirits came, spirits which would become plants, animals and the elements.

When the Ancestors' song was done, they lay to rest once more. They became the sky, seas and land. Today, their descendants still use ancient paths across the landscape known as 'songlines'.

This Australian Aboriginal story tells us how the world came to be.

All religions have some kind of creation myth. Some religions have several. After all, humans like to know *why* things are. Who made the sun, the moon and the stars? In a pre-scientific age, religion was the only answer you had.

Creation myths often reflect the cultures from which they come. For instance, many Aboriginal Australians were nomadic, hence the importance of the 'songlines'. Consider also one Shinto myth which echoes Japan's maritime history. Here the world was formed after two divine siblings churned up the celestial seas with magic spears. As their spears dripped, the puddles formed Japan's islands. Then there's the gore-loving Vikings. In Norse mythology, Odin and his brothers murder the giant Ymir. His blood becomes the sea, his flesh the ground, his skull the sky and his broken bones the mountains. Lovely.

Many creation myths mimic the very real creation stories we see in nature. For example, both the Chinese Pangu and the Hindu Brahma are believed to have emerged from some cosmic egg. And, of course, there's a lot of divine sex too. In Maori mythology, Rangi and Papa get it on. For the Babylonians, Apsu and Tiamet 'mingled their waters', while in the Aztec version, Cōātlīcue is impregnated, surprisingly, by a great ball of feathers.

The monotheistic myths – of a single God creating the world in six days – are unique in being 'ex nihilio', meaning a creation out of nothing. Most other myths involve gods working on some pre-existing celestial material to sculpt the world. The Abrahamic myths involve simply God saying a thing and it being so. Which is what you'd expect from an all-powerful deity, I suppose.

Creation myths are essential to the human need to know. While the Big Bang theory does, no doubt, have its own magic, I do lament the loss of creation stories. It would be nice to see some giant ribs on a country walk.

Ancestral Worship
Those Who Have Gone Before

To worship something is to appreciate it. It's to put that thing on a pedestal, call it sacred and label it as more important than anything. Worshipping some*one* tells the universe that this person matters and that you are devoted to them. It's no surprise, then, that one of the first forms of religious worship recorded was of our dead relatives. In life, our parents and family are the magnetic pole about which we spin. When we lose them, it feels like we're falling – the world suddenly seems a much scarier, uncertain and lonely place.

As far back as ancient Egypt and Mesopotamia, we see evidence of ancestor veneration. It's a practice likely as old as humanity. In the nineteenth century, the anthropologist Herbert Spencer argued that ancestral worship was the early precursor to all of the more complex religions that came after.

Ancestral worship depends upon the assumption that we have a soul or spirit that lives on after we die. These spirits would never stray far, however. If you needed help getting pregnant, or the crops were having a hard year, or your gammy leg wasn't getting better, you could call upon your ancestral spirits to help. Of course, being as mercurial as their former, corporeal selves, they were also known to be vengeful or spiteful. In the Japanese folk story *The Tale of Genji* (see page 253), one of Genji's old, jealous (and deceased) lovers returns to possess and kill Genji's pregnant wife.

Most cultures had some form of ancestral worship. In some, only recently dead ancestors or close family members were revered. In others, heads of tribes or founding fathers were the most devoutly worshipped. For the Greeks, Vikings, Celts, Teutons and Slavic peoples, ancestor worship heavily overlapped with hero worship – with the tales and sagas of great legends becoming more and more embellished with each retelling.

Over time, and for a lot of the world, ancestral worship was superseded by the major religions, especially monotheism (see page 282). But, as with all primal, ancient practices, these things rarely go away. Today, roughly 15 per cent of people claim to see or hear their dead loved ones. Ancestral worship remains strong in a lot of sub-Saharan Africa and rural India. In Japan and China, there's great respect, remembrance and reverence given to dead relatives (even if we might not call it fully fledged *worship*). In modern China, the Confucian virtue of filial piety is enjoying a resurgence.

The need to be close to our loved ones doesn't go away when they die. The security, support and happiness they give us in life cannot be replaced easily, if ever. So, ancestral worship is a basic human desire. It's a natural response to a cold, indifferent and difficult world. It's probably how religions first started.

Pantheism
There Is Only One

There's a memorable scene at the end of *The Matrix* when the hero, Neo, now blessed with the ability to see the world for what it is, witnesses the numbers that make up the universe. He sees the walls, doors and people as just modifications of the same underlying code. As with all great science fiction, the science isn't *that* fictitious. What Neo sees is really not that far removed from how the world actually is. Rather than green digits, we know the world is made up of atoms (or string – see page 86). You, this book, the sun and the distant aliens laughing at us over their breakfast are all made of the same stuff. We are all one.

It's great when science and religion come together like this. After all, the idea that 'everything is one' is a very old idea indeed.

In the eighteenth century, the Irish philosopher John Toland gave us the word 'pantheist', which means 'god in everything'. In its broadest understanding, it's the idea that God, the universe and our own consciousness are a single substance. We are God and God is us. Looking a bit more closely, though, we find there are quite a few kinds of pantheism.

'Panpsychism' is the idea that the entire universe, and everything within it, has a form of consciousness – there is a divine awareness in which we exist. 'Acosmic pantheism' is something seen in many Eastern religions – noticeably the Vedas of Hinduism and its offshoot, Buddhism. This is the belief that the world as we see it is simply one of appearances (or 'maya'). The world as we encounter it is fake and the *real* world is the divine order that lies behind this illusory veil. Finally, there's a kind of mysticism that is seen on the peripheries of most major religions (and many smaller ones, too). While monotheists will vehemently reject the label of pantheism, the broader idea that 'we are all part of God' is rarely far from any theological history.

In philosophy, there's one big pantheistic name, and that is the seventeenth-century Dutch Jew Baruch Spinoza. Spinoza argued that there could only be one underlying substance to everything, so when we use the words 'me' or 'God', we're just using two names for the same thing. He argued that the reason we see the world as made up of discrete, detached objects has nothing to do with the *truth* of reality but is down to our own myopic condition.

Pantheism is simultaneously very weird and pretty common sense. It's weird because people who say we are part of some 'universal consciousness' often also enjoy LSD and wear bandanas. Yet it's common sense because the more you learn about the sciences, the more unity you find. Perhaps we are all simply the current manifestation of a fundamental substance?

Ghosts
A Very Old Spook

Olive is a rational, scientifically minded atheist. She has no time for God, thinks metaphysics is nonsense and scoffs at the idea of life after death. Olive believes in nothing beyond the physical, explicable world of science.

... And yet, Olive is scared of ghosts. She won't call them that, perhaps, but creaks in the night terrify her, and she's pretty sure someone – or *something* – watches her in the dark.

Believing in ghosts is a staple of the human psyche. They are the restless, dissatisfied wraiths of the liminal who, like us all, simply want to find a home.

Ghosts – or ghost stories – are as old as the first dark and stormy night. In the unseen blackness beyond the firepit, all manner of spirits are imaginable. The idea of a soul goes back at least as far as ancient Egypt (called *Ka*) so it's not a great leap to believe some of these souls might wander or get lost. Almost all cultures have a 'psychopomp' – a mythical figure, like the Grim Reaper, who escorts the freshly deceased across the shadowy borderlands to their final destination. But of course a few troubled souls are bound to hotfoot it away.

A ghost is a symbol of unfulfilled purpose. Ghosts are not *meant* to wander the worldly plane, so they must be here for a reason. Often this is to cause havoc. It might be as harmless as a poltergeist hiding your salt cellar or it might be a vengeful spirit intent on murder. Ghosts are the bringers of sickness, misfortune and death, which is why we still perform all manner of superstitious actions to ward off evil spirits. In most myths and stories that feature ghosts, once the cause of the spirits' dissatisfied roaming is resolved, they can return to whatever Elysium or Sheol awaits them.

Of course, as both Islam and Christianity are monotheistic religions (see page 282), there isn't much room for ghosts. But you cannot easily purge such a deeply rooted, primal belief. Formally, there are no ghosts in Christian theology – but when you have demons possessing bodies and angels hovering about to intervene, it sounds quite ... ghostly. Likewise, in Islam, the Quran explicitly mentions jinn – good or bad spirits that can be metaphorical or very real depending on who you ask.

Today, ghosts are part of our collective folk psychology. Mediums and psychics sell out huge festival halls with their promise of talking to spirits. Horror movies bring in billions of dollars, and Halloween is a social highlight of the year. Most of us know of our cultural ghost stories – be it Anne Boleyn in the Tower of London, the phantom of Okiku's well in Japan or the Bell Witch from Tennessee. However rational we might be, most people will feel at least a little uncomfortable in the dark – for there roam spirits, spectres and shades.

Monotheism

The One, True God

The world is a profusion of wonder. We are touched by a sense of awe when we gaze at an early-evening moon, experience the sway of a windy forest, hear the jabble of an ocean. It's there in all those forces and powers to which we're viscerally aligned, even if we're only dimly conscious of it. It's easy to see why the human imagination began to see spirits in these forces. Polytheism – the belief that there are many gods – comes naturally to us. The earliest records we have show people worshipping entire pantheons. Egypt, Babylon, Greece, Rome, China, Mesoamerica – they all had legions of deities.

Which is why monotheism is such a curiosity. For many of us, born into the twenty-first century, monotheism is the norm. But for much of human history, it would have been unthinkable nonsense.

Monotheism is an anomaly in the history of ideas, because it largely comes out of nowhere. You do have the Brahman in Hinduism as the one god, source of all life and lesser gods, and ancient Egyptian mythology also hints at a single source of creation, but these are more like chief or creator deities than monotheistic gods, *per se*. Monotheism as we understand it – one, all-powerful God (with a capital letter) who precludes all others – only really bursts onto the scene with the Jews in the middle of the first millennium BCE.

Before monotheism, gods had to have a certain success rate if they were to survive the test of time. If a fertility god never gave you children, or the god of fish kept your nets empty, they'd be abandoned as quickly as an uncharged smartphone.

The God of the Jews was supposed to be a tribal war god who promised victory to his acolytes and worshippers. But He was awful at it. The Old Testament is a page-by-page account of the Jews' defeat, despair and humiliations. But the strange thing is that the Jews *didn't* ditch Yahweh. *Au contraire* – they doubled down. In their various exiles and under all manner of hardships, they stubbornly, determinedly, faithfully stood by their God. In fact, they continued to preach that their God was the *only* God. It wasn't His fault all these bad things happened; it must be theirs.

If the Jews started and kept alive the idea of monotheism, the Christians took it mainstream. The Jews were very protective of their religion and had tricky dietary (and genital) entry requirements. Christianity, though, was open to everyone. It was also popular with the Roman army, so it spread quickly across the Roman Empire and thus into Europe.

Today, the majority of the world's religious are monotheists. They are the Muslims, Jews and Christians whose mosques, synagogues and churches dominate our cities. Not bad for an idea that once belonged only to a tiny, downtrodden, enslaved minority who wandered homeless for seventy years.

Hell

Sado-voyeurism

There's a macabre allure to Hell. Whether it be a big-budget CGI scene out of Hollywood, the epic good vs. evil war of Milton's *Paradise Lost* or the schadenfreude description of Inferno in Dante's *Divine Comedy*, we are fascinated by damnation. We love the fire and brimstone, the gnashing of teeth, the pitchforks and horns, and that Rolling Stones song. Yet in the grand scheme of human history, the idea is peculiarly recent, and it owes much to apocalyptic (see page 297) Christian texts and thinkers.

The idea of Hell as a place to inhabit for eternity comes from those tragedy-loving Greeks. In their account, for the majority of the dead the afterlife was simply grey and drab. When Homer recounts Odysseus visiting Hell, he meets Achilles and Agamemnon complaining only about how bored they are. It comes over as a bit like an empty airport, with only arrivals coming in. A pretty accurate description of Hell, for some, but not awful.

And, in some ways, this is similar to the Jewish understanding of Hell, or Sheol, which is better translated as 'grave'. It's a place of 'worms and dust', beneath the earth.

Hell really starts to get exciting with Christianity. Around the third century AD, about the time St Paul was writing, people started converting. Christian preachers went into proselytising overdrive, and fear is a powerful weapon. The imagery of Hell became a great tool to persuade non-believers of the importance of looking to their souls. And this reached its apogee in Dante Alighieri (c. 1265–1321).

Dante's *Inferno* has the Roman poet Virgil act as our tour guide on a sado-voyeuristic sightseeing tour of Hell. Each level gets progressively crueller, and the worse your sin, the lower you go. These nine levels go right to the core of Earth, where lives the three-headed Satan, feasting on Brutus, Cassius and Judas (interestingly, Satan lies entombed in ice, and not fire). Each type of sinner faces their own poetic judgement. Thieves metamorphose into snakes; false counsellors are whipped by fiery tongues; seducers are buried in faeces; corrupt statesmen are thrown into boiling tar.

Writers and artists after Dante, from Milton to Bosch, depicted Hell in ever more gruesome ways. Yet as the centuries moved on, Hell morphed from a physical place of never-ending torment to a psychological metaphor for great anguish. William Blake, for instance, reinterpreted Milton's Hell as a metaphor for the spiritual absence of God, whilst today, many liberal Christians see Hell as a figurative or even psychoanalytic concept. The French philosopher Jean-Paul Sartre said, 'Hell is other people.'

The idea of Hell is a powerful one. It has terrified millions of believers and it has dominated literature and art for millennia. And it's no doubt true that the horrified fascination we feel when imagining Hell is often far more alluring than Heaven.

The Way, or the Dao
Go with the Flow

Do you ever feel like something's wrong? It might be a partner, a job or even a new book you're not enjoying. It's that feeling where everything's a chore. Everything requires monumental effort just to keep going. When we feel this way, the wisdom of our age demands we fight and struggle. We are taught to see a barrier as something to be overcome. Our path is the right one, and the great people of history are those who never turn back.

But sometimes this is not the right path at all, and in Daoism we find another wisdom altogether. This feeling of struggle is a sure sign you've fallen from the Dao.

Lao Tzu is the semi-mythical founder of Daoism (or Taoism – the phoneme sounds somewhere between T and D to the non-native listener). Lao Tzu means 'Old Master', and it's unclear whether he was a single historical person or if this was a title given to a collection of sages and their works around the fifth century BCE. But what matters is Lao Tzu's influence, not least for the 20 million Daoists worldwide today, mainly in Asia, and the millions more throughout history.

The Dao translates as 'the Way' and is often compared to the flow of a river. Like a river, the Dao directs and carries all things, and we are like boats floating along its path. To row against the current is hard, and Daoism is the simple call to 'go with the flow' of the universe.

Daoism means finding harmony in life, and this involves letting the self mould to the world, like water fills a cup. You must adapt, compromise and take life as it comes, not as *you* try to force it to be. If your life is like a forest, the Dao is the wide, paved path. There may be other paths, but why struggle through thorns and thickets when life could be happy and easy? The *Daodejing*, the central text of Daoism, is a dense wonder of proverbs, wisdom and fables to guide the Daoist in finding this path.

A key element to Daoism is known as *wu wei*, or 'not doing'. It's not an excuse for a duvet day and Netflix binge. In fact, it's often the very opposite; *wu wei* is to recognise and accept the pull of forces far greater than us. It's to walk the path that opens up. In the same way that Islam means 'surrender' to the power of Allah, *wu wei* is to surrender to the great currents of the Dao. It is to take action – but not by our plan.

The simple wisdom of Daoism is that if something feels wrong, chances are it is. Faced with life's obstacles, Lao Tzu teaches us to be more like the river and let ourselves wash over and around them. True happiness, the Dao, is to find our path in life – the path that feels right.

Prayer
Theocommunication

The Austrian psychiatrist Thomas Szasz once said, 'If you talk to God, you are praying; if God talks to you, you have schizophrenia.' It's a funny observation about a serious issue, and there is a genuine question lurking beneath it. Prayer is meant to be the communication between humans – profane, physical and infuriatingly mortal as we are – and the divine, however that's understood. With such drastically different participants, how can we understand that idea of 'communication' at all?

Perhaps it's better (and far less theologically complex) to focus on prayer from the human side of things. Given that prayer, or some kind of petitioning of the supernatural, is a universal and ancient human tradition, it well deserves its place in this book.

Broadly speaking, we can divide prayer into three different types: magic, worship and therapy.

Almost all prayers in recorded history involve an element of magic. For most religious believers in the world today – from Catholics in Rome to animists around the River Omo – prayer has to be magical. If there was not even the slightest prospect of divine intervention, then prayer would be a lifeless, pointless thing. If nothing comes of praying, then it's just words in the wind. Despite priestly exhortations and imams' protestations, a lot of believers *do* expect God or some kind of divinity to intervene on their behalf. They want miracle healing, divine retribution and supernatural meddling.

But if prayer is *only* about magic then the more mystical element of belief is lost. Court wizards and tribal shamans are useful and important but they are not worthy of worship. And so, prayer also has to have elements of adoration, humility and dependency. Thanksgiving is one example – the Ainu of Japan give thanks to a god or gods (called *kamuy*) before every meal. In Bantu and some Chinese ancestral worship (see page 277), prayer is simply adoration or respect-giving. Songs of worship, rituals of gratitude and everyday acknowledgements of a divinity are all essential to the worship part of prayer.

Then there's the third element: therapy. Sigmund Freud wasn't the first person in human history to realise that talking things over is good for you. When we externalise our problems, and have someone listen in on our troubles, they seem just a little bit less of a burden. Even without the magical element acting as a kind of wishful get-out clause for life's woes, the act of prayer has huge, scientifically provable, therapeutic benefits.

Prayer is as popular today as it always has been because it makes us all feel better. It may be a form of magical thinking, but its effects are real.

Meditation
Find Your Centre

Take a moment to appreciate sitting down.

Find a good place and take a seat. Make sure your head and spine are straight but not stiff. Gently tuck your chin in. Shift your pelvis so you're not slouching forward, nor is your chest sticking out. Have you done it? It might feel uncomfortable but stay here for a moment. Take long, deep breaths. Let your mind go wherever it wants. Become aware of the sitting, and this alone.

Welcome to the Zen practice of *zazen* – or meditative sitting. It's one of a great many methods humans have developed to still the mind, enjoy a moment and let the weary take a break.

The word 'Zen' has mysterious, New Age connotations, but the word is only a Japanese translation of the Chinese *chan*, which means meditation. Whilst almost all schools of Buddhism have some form of meditation, Zen is the branch that places the focus mostly, even exclusively, on it.

There are, broadly, three types of Zen meditation. The first is a mindfulness of breathing. The second is to reflect on the famous riddles of the Kōan ('what is the sound of one hand clapping?' kind of thing). The third is known as *zazen*, which means 'just sitting'.

In Hindu traditions, meditation is understood as yoga. Yoga is the umbrella term for any discipline that seeks to train the mind – usually through meditation or contemplation. It's the deliberate effort to overcome all those disturbances in our thoughts – to bring stillness, mindfulness and calm. How we do that depends on which school of yoga we belong to. The common Western understanding of yoga today – the one involving gyms, health classes and expensive island retreats – actually arrived relatively late to the yoga party. This physical, gymnastic kind of yoga is known as hatha yoga, owing itself to Swatmarama around the fifteenth or sixteenth century.

Most of us imagine meditation to be the reserve of bearded monks and yoga as the pastime of elastic-limbed contortionists. But any conscious effort to steer or still the mind is technically meditation. Taking a deep breath and slowly letting it out is Zen. Going for a long run after work is meditation. A long, groaning stretch after a day in front of a screen is yoga.

It just so happens that over the millennia various cultures have developed the most effective techniques to clear the head. The mind is a wonderful, powerful thing – but it can be loud and it can be exhausting. Sometimes it's necessary just to press the mute button for a while, to recharge and to reset. Meditation is the accumulated advice of the many millions who've done just that.

Incarnation
Bridges to the Divine

Imagine being an actual *god* and then, one day, waking up in a human body. Presumably your entire existence has previously involved wobbling about as some kind of metaphysical, heavenly ether and getting your way ... about everything. Now you've got to go to the bathroom, wait for the bus and deal with idiot humans who think you're mad. But you've got a job to do and a species to save. You'll take one for Team Divinity.

Almost all world religions, across all recorded history, have some kind of 'incarnation' event, where divinity is made flesh. For most faiths, it's the ultimate act of sacrifice – a god coming down to our level.

The oldest stories we have, such as the *Epic of Gilgamesh*, the *Iliad* or the earliest books of the Old Testament, all have gods walking among us. In the *Iliad*, the gods will just stroll into a scene, pushing pieces around willy-nilly, caring not one jot about *deus ex machina* clichés. In the Book of Genesis in the Bible, an angel takes earthly form to wrestle with Jacob – 'until daybreak' – while the Angel of the Lord appears many times to instruct the chosen people in this or that, most famously as a burning bush.

In the Hindu tradition, incarnation is a foundational pillar of belief. The god Vishnu is said to have taken on ten 'avatars', like Rama or Krishna. Each divine avatar has a specific purpose – usually to restore some cosmic imbalance or to avenge a previous defeat in battle. In Buddhism, *re*incarnation is the tenet that all living things are locked in the cycle of *samsara*, whereby the metaphysical 'mindstream' is encased in a new body after death. In Mahayana Buddhism, a *bodhisattva* is one who has attained enlightenment and *could* release their being in *nirvana* but has instead decided to reincarnate as a spiritual leader or guide – sacrificing nirvana for the benefit of all sentient life.

But the idea of incarnation is most often associated, in the West, with the Christianity of the New Testament. Jesus of Nazareth is professed to be 'God made flesh'. God the Father sent his own Son (who is also Himself – it's a trinitarian puzzle) to act as the sacrificial lamb to absolve mankind from our Edenic fall from grace. Up to the Council of Chalcedon, held in 451 CE, there was a debate among Christians about the nature of Jesus. Arianism, a rival theology (later declared heresy), believed that Jesus was an inferior thing altogether. He wasn't God incarnate but something God-like. Today, orthodox Christian belief has Jesus as both *wholly* God and *wholly* human – a paradox requiring a great deal of doxastic acrobatics and late-night debate.

Incarnation is huge in theology. It is the moment a god understands what it is like to be human. The divine can experience our narrow but beautifully unique vantage point. When they do so, they *humanise* their religion. They act as the bridge and conduit between our prosaic lives and the majesty of the Infinite.

Atheism
We Don't Do God

Atheism is a difficult concept. On one level, it's as simple as its etymological roots – 'a' meaning 'no' or 'without' and 'theism' meaning 'belief in a God'. So, atheists are those who do not believe in a god. Yet it's overly simplistic to assume this describes all atheists. Especially if you consult the history books. In most European, pre-modern sources, if someone was accused of atheism, it meant simply non-Christian. Hindus, Buddhists, Shinto practitioners and all manner of indigenous believers might be called atheists. To understand atheism, then, we have to dig a little deeper.

A good place to start is China. On first impressions, it is a notably non-religious country – over 90 per cent of Chinese adults claim to be atheists. Yet, on closer inspection, things are more confusing. Seventy per cent of these same adults also engage in some form of ancestor worship (see page 276). Likewise, the vast majority of the country practises the quasi-religious practice of traditional Chinese medicine (see page 94). In China, atheism is interpreted more as 'not of one of the major religions'.

Today, most people understand atheism in the Richard Dawkins kind of way. This is to say, atheists are people who simply reject certain belief statements such as 'Jesus healed the sick', 'Allah created the world', or 'some yogis can fly'. They deny the existence of God and gods. Yet this kind of atheism is a very modern, hugely minority worldview – smaller still, if we take on a historical lens.

Many in the developed post-Enlightenment world today do not appreciate just how central religion was to most people throughout most of history. People would invoke various superstitions (like 'touch wood') not out of quaint habit but because they actually thought it would prevent evil spirits from appearing. A local church, gurdwara or mosque would be the beating heart of a community – and their religious leaders would be authority, advice-giver and support base rolled into one. Up until the seventeenth century, everything was seen in terms of God or gods.

But atheism as a formal rejection of God went hand in hand with the Enlightenment and scientific revolution. When European philosophers elevated humans and human reason to the most important thing in the universe, it naturally demoted God a bit. Humanism meant humans were the centre of things, not religion. In Voltaire, David Hume and Friedrich Nietzsche, we find philosophers pouring scorn on traditional religion. In the French Revolution and for Karl Marx, it's seen as getting in the way.

Today, we are no less complicated than our ancestors. Atheism is ostensibly on the rise but religious belief is not dwindling. A great many people who call themselves atheists still believe in ghosts, karma, an afterlife, fate, 'manifesting' or angels. It goes to show how difficult the term 'atheist' actually is.

Apocalypse
The End Is Always Nigh

The Book of Revelation is the black sheep of the New Testament. Whilst St Paul does have his nasty moments, the general theme of Christianity is one of love, forgiveness and charity. Why, then, does the Bible finish with the Whore of Babylon drinking the blood of saints, ocean dragons battling archangels, broken vials pouring festering sores and fiery agony onto mankind and, of course, the Four Horsemen of the Apocalypse? It's all rather at odds with the tender, kind and gentle carpenter's son who's meant to be the Messiah.

Yet the Book of Revelation, and the idea of the apocalypse generally, came to dominate Christianity and popular culture far more than any other book of the Bible. It even defined how we view the universe.

Many of us born into the Western intellectual tradition can't help but see time as linear. There's a beginning, an end, and we're all caught somewhere in the middle. Yet this vision owes much to the Book of Revelation. Having a fire-and-brimstone apocalypse acting as the full stop to all history gives meaning to the whole. If there's an end of time, it puts into perspective the sense of journey that we're on.

And it all stems from the idea of apocalypse. There's something about the concept of a vengeful Day of Judgement that captures the imagination, with its implicit threat of 'you'll pay for this'. The origins of apocalyptic literature in the Old Testament began around the time of the Jewish exile in Babylon. When it became clear that their defeated enslavement wasn't ending soon, the Jewish prophets like Isiah and Ezekiel turned to apocalyptic writing, which was hugely cathartic for God's supposedly chosen people.

Ever since, the idea of God's Final Judgement has soothed the oppressed. The Book of Revelation acts as a kind of Rorschach inkblot in which you can paint your earthly enemies as the diabolical defeated at Armageddon. And, in fact, it's almost a sociological rule that the more a community is persecuted, the more they turn to apocalyptic thinking. The Jews in Babylon, the early Christians under Rome, the Protestants under Catholicism, the Catholics under Protestantism, the pilgrims in America and pretty much everyone during times of plague – yep, COVID-19 might actually have been the Pale Horse. Even Revelation itself was thought to be written by a disgruntled exile taking aim at the Turkish Church.

Of course, the other reason the Apocalypse has made such a big impact on our culture is that dragons, celestial battlegrounds and a horned beast make for pretty interesting reading. Bored schoolkids will always flip to that over a forty-year migration in the desert.

Acknowledgements

If you step outside of your comfort zone, it pays to get a bit of extra help. After all, it's a silly man who decides to climb a mountain or hike through the jungle with some tatty trainers and a ten-year-old penknife. Luckily for me, I'm blessed with a truck's worth of help. The 'comfort zone' for me was my previous book *Mini Philosophy*, and stepping outside that into the baffling lab-lands of physics, biology and chemistry was risky business. What I needed was people who make their homes in those lab-lands, and my uncontained and unreserved thanks must go to them.

Dave Roche is as smart as he is kind and genuine. If the Dalai Lama and Marie Curie mingled their waters, Dave would be the result. Dave edited all my science sections, and he often put me right, but he did so with the soft, patient tone of a teacher telling a student he's trying hard but is an idiot.

Fabian Ruehle is probably the most intelligent person I know. He has more degrees than I have matching socks, and if Marvel ever cast Mr Fantastic (widely acknowledged as the brainiest guy in all of the Marvel Universe), then they need to look up Fabi. Thanks to Fabi for diving into the unfathomable depths of physics that few people know.

Beth Watts is a new mum, and so the fact she took the time to help with my biology and chemistry sections shows that she is not only ridiculously generous and insanely intelligent but also possessed of an adamantine backbone. If changing nappies isn't bad enough, then reading Jonny Thomson interchangeably using 'element' and 'chemical' will give any masochist the kicks they want.

Finally, Andrew Davies has literally written textbooks on biology. He's an internationally renowned expert in the field, and so when he offered to look over my biology section, it was rather like getting Steven Spielberg to look at a video of me dancing drunkenly at a Christmas party. But Andrew's comments were perfect – detailed, gentle and encouraging.

But however great all of my friends have been, they, at least, had to endure only one or a few of my chapters. My editor, Lindsay Davies, had to do the whole lot. As ever, she's been patient, kind and genuine and her edits are always both good-natured and insightful. If I had a penny for every time she'd found a mistake, I'd have enough money to send her on the Indian yoga retreat she so desperately deserves.

Thanks, too, to Charlie, my agent, for being the kind of steadfast, background support everyone needs. Thanks also to Wildfire, who thought another round of *Mini* would be a good thing. I hope/fully expect it will make millionaires out of us all.

Finally, and as always, I am indescribably grateful to the huge mesh of friends and family who support me in this, and always. My boys, Freddie and Charlie, have been utterly useless when it comes to this book but they give reason and happiness to every day. Mum, Dad, Jamie, James, Hagi, Jonny, Bex, Amanda, Roman and Ann have all been there to bounce ideas around as much as bounce Charlie around, too. But none of this would be possible without Tanya. Not only has Tanya taken on the great lion's share of crap (literally and metaphorically) of child-rearing while I tap away in the study, but she is what makes everything feel fuller. Tanya is what turns a house into a home and a day into a memory. She makes life life. I love her so much.

Index

Index

Index